9/11

TRUTH UNTOLD ©

EPIC FINDINGS, HEROES, AND MIRACLES OF ALL 9/11 EVENTS

Troy Clark, Ph.D.

troyclark.net

amazon.com/author/troyclark

TROY CLARK

9/11

TRUTH UNTOLD

"I recommend this book"
Manuel Chea
9/11/2001 Survivor, World Trade Center North Tower, 49th Floor

More publications by Dr. Troy Clark: (paperback, eBook, audiobook)
amazon.com/author/troyclark

Online retail outlets:
Kindle, Barnes-n-Noble Nook, Apple iBookstore, Goodreads.com, BookDaily.com, Sony Reader, Kobo, Palm Doc, Diesel, CreateSpace.com, Smashwords, Audible.com, Apple iTunes, Oyster, Scribd, OverDrive, Flipkart, Bookworld, Indigo, Buy.com.
Aldiko & Stanza (mobile apps)

Special Recommendation

I was greatly interested when Dr. Clark asked me to review a book about 9/11 that he was writing.

Over the years I have found Dr. Clark to be a man of integrity and a God fearing person, so I had no doubt that he would do justice to "another" 9/11 book.

Though I cannot agree with some of the 9/11 theories that have been reported, Dr. Clark does a masterful job presenting all sides objectively allowing each reader to determine for themselves truth from falsehood.

Every historical event has had its share of speculations and conspiracy theories. Events like the assassination of President John F. Kennedy and the first landing on the moon are rife with conspiracy theories. 9/11 is no different, and there is no denying that these speculations do exist and have become a part of the 9/11 narrative.

I found the chapter on "9/11 History" fascinating. This chapter is not just background history on the events of the 9/11/2001 attacks, but also about other events that happened on the date 9/11 over a couple of millennia. The 9/11 poems chapter was both moving and inspiring, and I loved this chapter very much.

Ultimately, the worth of a book is based on whether it glorifies God. Scripture tells us in 1 Corinthians 10:31 that whatever you do, do it all for the glory of God. This book certainly does.

On that basis alone, I recommend this book to you.

Manuel Chea

9/11/2001 Survivor, World Trade Center North Tower, 49th Floor

Dedicated to

3,000+ souls who perished, and 6,000+ people treated
in area hospitals as a result of 9/11/2001

Family members and friends of all victims

First responders, caretakers, and volunteers,
who bravely served the wounded in aftermath horror

New York Mayor Rudy Giuliani,
who demonstrated clear leadership in national tragedy

President George W. Bush,
who gravely fought back ensuring America's future safety

All US military and intelligence personnel who defeat and
stop Koran-inspired terror around the globe

Table of Contents

Introduction

Do you remember where you were - what you were doing - when you first heard it?.. *"Apparently, a plane has crashed into a World Trade Center Tower..We're not sure how, or why, this has happened.."*

National news outlets in breaking coverage scrambled to make sense of it with several different speculations. Some said an errant piper cub veered off course in high winds. Some said it wasn't a plane at all, but a bomb exploded inside the building. Some talked of a gas leak being explored a couple blocks away by New York City Fire Department.

Then, 16 minutes after the first crash, at 9:02am ET, with America's collective eye trained on real-time TV images of dark smoke billowing out of a new mouth on the North Tower backdropped against a blue sky, a 2nd commercial airliner inconceivably plunges smack-dab into the heart of the South Tower at full throttle in a fireball explosion of widespread death and panic.

The nation was taken aback in horror with a collective gasp, not believing what we were seeing with our own eyes, feeling shock, gripped in angst, and soon thereafter, fear and anger, begging surreal questions of - *"What's next?!"*

Here, it seeps in. America, yes, the United States of America, is being attacked on its own soil. We felt war.

Months after the 9/11/2001 tragedies, political pundits, Hollywood A-listers, ministers, and armchair philosophers, all grappled over fears Americans wanted satisfied:

Why did this happen?
How were we so ill-prepared to see it coming, or stop it?
Is America safe now?
What events may have led to this tragedy?
How can we prevent this from ever happening again?

This book attempts to satisfy these questions, and much more, as we piece together a more complete picture of the whole story of 9/11.

The fight for freedom never ends

Chapter One

Pre 9/11 Events

9/11 was a deliberate, carefully planned evil act of the long-waged war on the west by Koran-inspired soldiers of Allah around the world.[1]

Michelle Malkin

Political Commentator, Author, Conservative Blogger

Islamic terrorist attacks on the US leading up to 9/11/2001:
1979 –US Embassy in Iran, 52 US Hostages (failed rescue attempt, Operation Eagle Claw, 8 servicemen dead, destruction of 2 US aircraft)
1983 – USMC Barracks bombing, Beirut, Lebanon (299 deaths)
1983 – US Embassy bombing, Beirut, Lebanon, (63 deaths)
1988 – Lockerbie, Scotland, Pan-Am Flight 103 to New York, bombed in flight (259 deaths)
1993 – NY World Trade Center bombing (6 deaths)
1996 – Saudi Arabia, Khobar Towers Military complex bombing (19 deaths)
1998 –US Embassy bombings in Tanzania and Kenya (200 deaths)
2000 – Yemen, USS Cole bombing (17 deaths)

February 23, 1998. Five radical caliphates (factions) of Islam signed a fatwa (Islamic Law to Holy War) calling on **all** Muslims of the world to unite against their perceived enemy of Islam by declaring war (jihad) against the United States of America. Signed by Sheikh **Usamah Bin-Muhammad Bin-Laden (Osama bin Laden)**, Ayman al-Zawahiri (leader of the Jihad Group in Egypt), Abu-Yasir Rifa'I Ahmad Taha (leader of the Islamic Group), Sheikh Mir Hamzah (secretary of the Jamiatul-Ulema-e-Pakistan), and Fazlul Rahman (leader of the Jihad Movement in Bangladesh), a partial segment of the text reads:

The U.S. has been occupying the lands of Islam in the holiest of places....The best proof of this is their eagerness to destroy Iraq...their endeavor to fragment into paper statelets Saudi Arabia, Egypt, and Sudan....to guarantee Israel's survival and the occupation of the Peninsula. On that basis, and in compliance with Allah's order, we issue the following fatwa to all Muslims: The ruling to **kill the Americans** *and their allies-civilians and military-is an individual* **duty for every Muslim** *who can do it in any country in which it is possible to do it,...In accordance with the words of Almighty Allah, 'fight all pagans all together* **(surah 9:5)***....fight them until there is no more tumult, and there prevail justice and faith in Allah'.*[2]

Mohammed Atta, terrorist-pilot of American Airlines Flight 11 that crashed into the World Trade Center (WTC) North Tower, conceived the 9/11 terrorist attack in Hamburg, Germany, in 1998.

Known as "The Hamburg Cell," Atta, along with 3 other Islamic members, planned a jihad strike under the direction of Khalid Sheikh Mohammed. They met 3-4 times per week in a 3-bedroom apartment to discuss their anti-American and anti-Israeli views. They were convinced to join the al Qaeda network and wage jihad against America. They met with Osama bin Laden himself and swore their loyalty to him. Mohamed Atta was chosen by bin Laden as the leader of the group that would attack America. Atta would contact bin Laden several more times before the attacks. The men enrolled in a German flight training school, and later moved on to flight training schools in the United States at the recommendation of one of their instructors based in Germany.

Rudi Dekkers, a Dutch national and former owner of Huffman Aviation in Venice, FL, "unwittingly" trained terrorist hijackers Mohammed Atta and Marwan Al-Shehhi July 1 through Dec. 24, 2000. Once a $12M operation, now Dekkers is behind bars since 2012 for using his business as a criminal enterprise for shuttling illegal narcotics across the America border.

ABC news journalist John Miller wrote a passionate book about terrorist cells operating in America, *The Cell: Inside the 9/11 Plot, and why the CIA and FBI failed to stop it.* Miller estimates as many as 500 terrorist cells exist in the USA today. Miller was the first American journalist to interview Osama bin Laden, and has been tracking the story relentlessly since the 1993 WTC bombing.

USA Today article on 10/23/2015, *"Comey: Feds have roughly 900 domestic probes about Islamic State operatives, other extremists"* revealed FBI Director James Comey stated in an October 2015 speech to intelligence officials there are over 900 open investigations inside the US currently tracking ISIL-related operations (ISIL = Islamic State of Iraq and the Levant), *and* "other" US-based extremists.

ISIL seeks to expand its reach into the US, targeting largely young operatives through provocative social media campaigns denouncing traditional American military strength.

The film *Hamburg Cell* is a docudrama on the planning and execution of the 9/11 attacks. A co-production between Channel 4 in the UK and CBC in Canada, it was shown in the UK during September 2004 amid criticism that this was too close to the anniversary of the attack.

A purported theory about Mohammad Atta is widespread online:

Terrorist pilot Mohammed Atta blew up a bus in Israel in 1986. The Israelis captured, tried and imprisoned him. As part of the Oslo agreement with the Palestinians in 1993, Israel had to agree to release so-called "political prisoners." However, the Israelis would not release any with "blood on their hands." The American President at the time, Bill Clinton, and his Secretary of State, Warren Christopher, "insisted" that all prisoners be released. Thus Mr. Atta was freed, and eventually thanked the US by flying an airplane into Tower One of the World Trade Center.

This was reported by American TV networks at the time that the terrorists were first identified. It was censored in the US from all official reports.

Israel officially has denied the allegation, stating it was a different "Atta" responsible for opening fire inside a passenger bus with an Uzi machine gun, killing the driver and seriously wounding 3 others, who was later freed on legal technicalities; namely Mahmoud Atta, not Mohammad Atta.

Two years earlier, a federal report warned the Clinton Presidential administration that Osama bin Laden's terrorists were focusing on suicide hijacking of commercial airliners. *"Suicide bombers belonging to Qaeda's Martyrdom Battalion could crash-land an aircraft packed with high explosives into the Pentagon, the CIA, or the White House,"* the September 1999 report clearly explained.[3]

The report, **Sociology and Psychology of Terrorism: Who Becomes a Terrorist and Why?**, described the 9/11 suicide hijackings as a possible retribution for the inept Clinton-led 1998 US airstrike against bin Laden's "camps" in Afghanistan. **Operation Infinite Reach** was a hapless 1998 Clinton-led American cruise missile strike launched from American warships in the Red Sea onto several Al-Shifa pharmaceutical companies (aspirin factories).

The attack was lauded by adoring leftist mainstream media pundits as an administration's "best" response to the bombings of American embassies in Kenya and Tanzania just days earlier, killing 224 people (12 Americans), and injuring 5,000 others.

In reality, like Clinton himself, the strike was little more than a charade of whirling ineffectiveness.

The end results of **Operation Infinite Reach** were one confirmed kill of an innocent janitor, 10 wounded, *and* only succeeded in making matters worse in the region. The Sudanese Government demanded an apology from the Clinton administration, but none was ever offered.

Later, White House officials sheepishly acknowledged, thanks to intense and sustained conservative-talk-radio scrutiny of Clinton's sterile foreign policy decisions, *"the evidence that prompted President Clinton to order the missile strike on the Shifa plant was not as solid as first portrayed."* [4] Indeed, officials later said that there was **no proof** that the plant had been manufacturing nor storing nerve gas, nor had been linked to Osama bin Laden at all, who was a former resident of Khartoum in the 1990s.

At least George W. Bush possessed vetted documentation with 90% certainty of WMDs in Iraq before air strikes ever began the Iraq War. Yet, who was vehemently excoriated nightly by major news-related media outlets *CNN, NBS, CBS, NBC, MSNBC,* Colbert, Stewart, Maher, *SNL,* et al - - - Clinton or Bush?

Just hours before the 9/11/2001 terrorist attacks on the WTC Twin Towers, impeached President Bill Clinton is recorded in Australia stating braggadociously, *"I spent a lot of time thinking about him. And I nearly got him once.. I could have killed him* [Osama bin Laden].. *but I would have had to destroy a little town called Kandahar in Afghanistan and kill 300 innocent women and children, and then I would have been no better than him. And so I didn't do it."* [5]

Hear the full recordings online:

abcnews.go.com/US/bill-clinton-hours-911-attacks-killed-osama-bin/story?id=24801422
reuters.com/article/2014/08/01/us-usa-clinton-binladen-idUSKBN0G14J720140801

Looking for a plausible excuse to avoid conflict instead of taking decisive action, was Clinton totally unaware of drone strikes, or Navy Seal options? Of course, he knew Osama could be killed without having to *"destroy an entire town."*

Osama bin Laden years later would be permanently marginalized without any loss of innocent life, thanks to the Bush-led War on Terror policy carried out by Obama to terminate the known terrorist by a Special Forces operation. Clinton simply offered lame-duck action to divert attention away from his own unsuitability as Commander in Chief.

The *9/11 Commission Report* recounts an episode in December 1998 where Clinton's administration considered a cruise missile strike opportunity to actually kill Osama bin Laden, the Saudi Arabian founder of al Qaeda, after learning he would be in Kandahar. The strike was cancelled because of a tepid "fear" that "perhaps" 300 others might be killed or injured, the report says. According to the official report, the missed chance made several high ranking officials reasonably livid.

Clinton, again, considered a missile strike against bin Laden laid out before him in May 1999, but as was the case months prior, he decided to hold back from striking, wary of alleged "conflicting" intelligence reports.

Clinton left the Presidential office sullied and disgraced about nine months before the September 11, 2001, terrorist attacks on US soil; proclaiming to have "seriously" focused on Osama bin Laden, the mastermind of US embassy bombings in Tanzania and Kenya in 1998 that killed more than 200 people, including 12 Americans.

There is one thing that makes society feel unsafe more than English Bobbies with a nightstick, and that is an elected liberal wielding national power. After 2001, Americans quickly caught up with the terminology and history of Koran-inspired terrorism, and realized several missed opportunities that may have prevented 9/11.

Millions of walking wounded from the hellacious aftermath of 9/11/2001 could have been conceivably averted except for the scandal-laden selfness of the previous Bill Clinton impeached presidency.

Strangely enough, a TV show pilot aired on March 4, 2001, depicted a terrorist plot to crash a commercial airliner into the World Trade Center Twin Towers. Killtown's program, *The Lone Gunman*, oddly "predicted" what would become reality 6 months before it actually happened.

The TV show footage is easily accessed online at YouTube:
https://www.youtube.com/watch?v=_rkrBCIBpdk
https://www.youtube.com/watch?v=G7YQrIx1bow
https://www.youtube.com/watch?v=vte0IkriKAc
http://killtown.911review.org/lonegunmen.html

In November 2002, Osama bin Laden brazenly published online an open "Letter to America", explaining his reason for the 9/11/2001 Islamic terrorist attack. The letter first appeared on the internet in Arabic and has since been translated and circulated by Islamists in Britain.

Written to the American people, the full letter contains a multitude of references to Allah (Muslim god) and specific Koran (Muslim bible) passages as Osama bin Laden's justifications for the 9/11 attacks on American soil.

You may read the full text online:
theguardian.com/world/2002/nov/24/theobserver

1979 US Embassy in Iran - 52 American Hostages (444 days):

Failed rescue attempt:

President Carter, US Hostages

1983 USMC Barracks bombing, Beirut, Lebanon (299 deaths):

1983 US Embassy bombing, Beirut, Lebanon, (63 deaths):

1988 Lockerbie, Scotland, Pan-Am Flight 103 to New York bombed in flight (259 deaths):

1993 New York World Trade Center bombing
(6 deaths / 1,000 wounded):

Ramzi Yousef   Mohammad Salameh   Abdul Yasin

1996 Saudi Arabia, Khobar Towers Military complex bombing (19 deaths):

1998 (2) US Embassy bombings Tanzania and Kenya (200 deaths):

Tanzania:

Kenya:

2000 Yemen, USS Cole bombing (17 deaths):

Hamburg cell, Germany:

Mohammed Atta, Khalid Sheikh Mohammed, Osama bin Laden:

Chapter Two

9/11/2001 Timeline

All of a sudden there were people screaming.
I saw people jumping out of the building. Their arms were flailing.
I stopped taking pictures and started crying.[1]

Michael Walters

Freelance photojournalist in Manhattan, NY, on 9/11/2001

TUESDAY, SEPTEMBER 11, 2001: [Eastern time]

12:00am: The United Nations International Day of Peace begins. New York election day primaries begin.

12:45am: Willie Brown, the Mayor of San Francisco gets a call from what he described as his airport security advising him that Americans should be cautious about their air travel on September 11th. Mayor Brown was scheduled to fly from San Francisco to New York City on September 11th.

6:45am: Two hours before the first attack, two workers at the instant messaging company Odigo receive messages warning of the WTC attack. This Israeli owned company headquarters is located two blocks from the WTC.

7:59am: American Airlines Flight 11, a Boeing 767-223ER with a maximum capacity of 181 passengers and 23,980 gallons of fuel, lifts off from Logan International Airport in Boston, Massachusetts, bound for Los Angeles International Airport in Los Angeles, California. Take-off was scheduled for 7:45am. There are supposed to be 92 passengers on board American Airlines Flight 11, yet when you add up the official death manifest list that was published on CNN.com, there are only 86 victims.

8:01am: United American Flight 93 is delayed for 40 minutes on the runway in Newark, NJ. The Boston Globe credits this delay as a major reason why this was the only one of the four flights not to succeed in its mission.

8:14am: United Airlines Flight 175, a Boeing 767-222 with a maximum capacity of 181 passengers and 23,980 gallons of fuel, lifts off from Logan International Airport in Boston, Massachusetts, bound for Los Angeles International Airport in Los Angeles, California. Take-off was scheduled for 7:58am. There are supposed to be 65 passengers on board, yet when you add up the official death manifest list that was published on CNN.com, there are only 56 victims.

8:19am: AA Flight 11 flight attendant Betty Ong uses a phone card to call AA Raleigh reservations center from seat 3R to report a possible hijacking and 2 attendants have been stabbed.
https://www.youtube.com/watch?v=icfkIH3j-nk

8:20am: American Airlines Flight 77, a Boeing 757-223 with a maximum capacity of 200 passengers and 11,489 gallons of fuel, lifts off from Dulles International Airport about 30 miles west of Washington, D.C. and the Pentagon, bound for Los Angeles International Airport in Los Angeles, California. Take-off was scheduled for 8:01am. There are supposed to be 64 passengers on board, yet when you add up the official death manifest list that was published on CNN.com, there are only 56 victims.

8:42am: United Airlines Flight 93, a Boeing 757-222 with a maximum capacity of 200 passengers and 11,489 gallons of fuel, lifts off from Newark International Airport in Newark, New Jersey bound for San Francisco International Airport, San Francisco, California. Take-off was scheduled for 8:01am. There are supposed to be 44 passengers on board, yet when you add up the official death manifest list that was published on CNN.com, there are only 33 victims.

8:43am: NORAD (North American Aerospace Defense Command) is notified that Flight 175 has been hijacked. Note: This means controllers working Flights 77 and Flight 93 would have been aware of Flight 175 and Flight 11 hijacking from this time.

8:46am: American Airlines Flight 11 impacts the north side of the North Tower of the WTC between the 93rd and 99th floors. American Airlines Flight 11 was flying at a speed of 490 miles per hour.

Approx 8:46am: According to NORAD command director Capt. Michael H. Jellinek, at some point not long after the WTC hit, telephone links are established with the National Military Command Center (NMCC) located inside the Pentagon, Canada's equivalent command center, Strategic Command, theater Cincs and federal emergency-response agencies. An Air Threat Conference Call is initiated. At one time or another, Bush, Cheney, Rumsfeld and key military officers are heard on the open line. [*Aviation Week and Space Technology*, 6/3/2002]

9:00am: A CIA training exercise run by the super secret NRO (National Reconnaissance Office) would simulate a small Lear jet crashing into a building just 20 miles from the Pentagon. The exercise is cancelled when an actual airliner crashes into the Pentagon just 5 minutes after the exercise started.

9:01am: United warns all of its aircraft of the potential for cockpit intrusion and to take precautions to barricade cockpit doors. Flight 93 pilots acknowledge the message. However, they're not told why, what happened at the WTC, or that another plane is missing.

9:02am: United Airlines Flight 175 impacts the south side of the South Tower of the WTC between the 78th and 84th floors at a speed of over 500mph. Parts of the plane including an engine leave the building from its north side, to be found on the ground up to six blocks away.

9:05am: Andrew Card walks up to and leans into President Bush's ear while he is listening to a story with 16 second graders in Sandra Kay Daniels' class at Emma E. Booker Elementary School in Sarasota, Florida. Card whispers in his ear, *"A second plane has hit the World Trade Center. America is under attack."* Bush remains calm and listens to the story with the students for at least 7 minutes: **youtube.com/watch?v=XR_rFXXz_44**

Between **8:47am** and **10:29am** many people trapped by fire and smoke in the upper floors of both World Trade Center towers, jumped to their deaths. One person at street level, a NYC Firefighter is hit by such a jumper and is also killed.

9:16am: The FAA (Federal Aviation Administration) informs NORAD that UA Flight 93 may have been hijacked. Hear the actual recordings online:
https://en.wikipedia.org/wiki/United_Airlines_Flight_93

(Before 9:27am) On UA Flight 93, at least three hijackers stand up and put red bandanas around their heads. Two of them force their way into the cockpit. One takes the loudspeaker microphone, apparently unaware it could also be heard by air traffic controllers, and announces that someone has a bomb onboard and the flight is returning to the airport. He tells them he is the pilot, but speaks with an accent.

9:27am: Flight 93 passenger, Tom Burnett, calls his wife, Deena, and says, *"I'm on United Flight 93 from Newark to San Francisco. The plane has been hijacked. We are in the air. They've already knifed a guy. There is a bomb on board. Call the FBI."* Deena connects to emergency 911. Deena wonders if the call might have been before the cockpit was taken over, because he spoke quickly and quietly as if he was being watched. He also had a headset like phone operators use, so he could have made the call unnoticed. This is the first of over 30 additional phone calls by passengers inside the plane.

9:28am: On United Airlines Flight 93 an open microphone aboard allows air traffic controllers to hear someone in the cockpit saying, *"Get out of here!"* The mike goes off and comes back on. Scuffling is heard in the background. Somebody again yells, *"Get out of here!"* Eventually there are a total of four murky radio transmissions, which include lots of non-English phrases: *"bomb on board"* twice, *"our demands"* and *"keep quiet"*.

9:30am: President Bush, speaking to the nation from Emma E. Booker Elementary School in Sarasota, Florida, says the country has suffered an *"apparent terrorist attack"* and *"a national tragedy"*. He assures America would chase down, *"those folks who committed this act"*. Bush also said, *"Terrorism against our nation will not stand."* It was an echo of *"This will not stand,"* the words his father, George H. W. Bush, had used a few days after Iraq invaded Kuwait in August 1990 - in George W. Bush's opinion, one of his father's finest moments.

9:31am: A hijacker on board Flight 93 can be heard on the cockpit voice recording ordering a woman to sit down. A woman, presumably a flight attendant, implores, *"Don't, don't,"* she pleads, *"Please, I don't want to die."* Patrick Welsh, the husband of flight attendant Debby Welsh, is later told that a flight attendant was stabbed early in the takeover, and it is strongly implied it was his wife. She was a first class attendant, and as Patrick says, *"knowing Debby, she would have resisted."*

9:32am: A hijacker says over the radio to Flight 93 passengers: *"Ladies and gentlemen, here it's the captain, please sit down. Keep remaining sitting. We have a bomb aboard."*

9:32am: Secret Service agents burst into Vice President Dick Cheney's White House office. They carry him under his arms, nearly lifting him off the ground, and take him to the security of the underground bunker in the White House basement.

9:32am: The New York Stock Exchange closed.

9:34am: Tom Burnett calls his wife Deena a second time. He says *"They're in the cockpit."* He has checked the pulse of the man who was knifed (later identified as Mark Rothenberg sitting next to him in seat 5B) and determined he is dead. She tells him about the hits on the WTC. He responds, *"Oh my God, it's a suicide mission."* As they continue to talk, he tells her the plane has turned back. By this time, Deena is in constant communication with the FBI, and a policeman is at her house.

9:35am: American Airlines begins landing all of its flights inside the United States.

9:37am: Jeremy Glick calls his wife Lyz from Flight 93. He describes the hijackers as Middle Eastern, Iranian looking. They put on red headbands and the three of them stood up and yelled and ran into the cockpit. He was sitting in the front of the coach section, but was sent to the back with most of the passengers. They claimed to have a bomb, which looked like a box with something red tied around it. He says the plane has turned around. Family members immediately call emergency 911 on another line. New York state police get patched in midway through the call. Glick finds out about the WTC towers. Two others onboard also learn about the WTC at about this time. Glick's phone remains connected until the very end of the flight.

9:37am: American Airlines Flight 77 is lost from radar screens and impacts the western side of the Pentagon. The section of the Pentagon hit consists mainly of newly renovated, unoccupied offices. The Pentagon says American Airlines Flight 77 hits them at **9:37am**.

9:39am: Flight 93 hijackers inadvertently transmit over the radio: *"Hi, this is the captain. We'd like you all to remain seated. There is a bomb on board. And we are going to turn back to the airport. And they had our demands, so please remain quiet."*

9:41am: Flight 93 passenger, Marion Birtton, calls a friend. She tells him two people have been killed, and the plane has been turned around.

Approx 9:41am: A few minutes after AA Flight 77 crashes, the Secret Service commands fighters from Andrews Air Force Base, 10 miles from Washington, to *"Get in the air now!"* Almost simultaneously, a call from someone else in the White House declares the Washington area "a free-fire zone." *"That meant we were given authority to use force, if the situation required it, in defense of the nation's capital, its property and people,"* says one of the pilots. Lt. Col. Marc H. (Sass) Sasseville, and a pilot only known by the codename "Lucky", sprint to their waiting F-16s armed only with "hot" guns and 511 rounds of "TP" non-explosive training rounds. The pilot later said that, had all else failed, they would have rammed into Flight 93. [*Aviation Week* and *Space Technology*, 9/9/02]

9:42am: United Airlines Flight 93 passenger Mark Bingham calls his mother. *"Mom, this is Mark Bingham,"* he said, nervously. *"I want to let you know that I love you. I'm calling from the plane. We've been taken over. There are three men that say they have a bomb."*

9:45am: From United Airlines Flight 93, Tom Burnett calls his wife Deena for the third time. She tells him about the crash into the Pentagon. Tom speaks about the bomb he'd mentioned earlier, saying, *"I don't think they have one, I think they're just telling us that."* He says the hijackers are talking about crashing the plane into the ground. *"We have to do something."* He says that he and others are making a plan. *"A group of us."*

9:45am to **9:58am:** UA Flight 93 passenger Todd Beamer tries to call his family but gets patched through to a Verizon supervisor. He said that the pilot and copilot were apparently dead, 2 hijackers were in the cockpit, one was guarding first class and another was guarding 27 passengers at the rear of the plane. He said that they have voted to storm the hijackers. The Verizon supervisor hears Todd Beamer before he hangs up, *"Are you guys ready? Let's roll."*

9:49am: The F-16s from Langley AFB finally arrive over Washington, D.C. to perform Combat Air Patrol over the city. It takes these F-16s 19 minutes to reach Washington, D.C. from Langley AFB which is about 130 miles to the south.

9:50am: Sandra Bradshaw calls her husband from Flight 93. She says, *"Have you heard what's going on? My flight has been hijacked. My flight has been hijacked with three guys with knives."* She tells him that they are in the rear galley filling pitchers with boiling water to use against the hijackers.

9:53am: The hijackers in the cockpit of Flight 93 grow concerned that the passengers might retaliate. One urges that the plane's fire ax be held up to the door's peephole to scare the passengers.

9:53am: The NSA intercepts a phone call from one of bin Laden's operatives in Afghanistan to a phone number in the Republic of Georgia. The caller says he has *"heard good news"* and that another target is still to come (presumably, Flight 93). CIA director George Tenet tells Defense Secretary Donald Rumsfeld about the intercept two hours later.

9:54am: Tom Burnett calls his wife, Deena, for the fourth and last time. In early reports of this call, he says, *"I know we're all going to die. There's three of us who are going to do something about it."* However, in a later and much more complete account, he sounds much more upbeat. *"It's up to us. I think we can do it. Don't worry; we're going to do something."* He specifically mentions they plan to regain control of the airplane over a rural area.

9:55am: President Bush arrives at the Sarasota-Bradenton International Airport and boards Air Force One.

9:55am: Inside his White House bunker, a military aide asks Cheney, *"There is a plane 80 miles out. There is a fighter in the area. Should we engage?"* Cheney immediately says, *"Yes."* As the fighter jet gets nearer to UA Flight 93, Cheney is asked the same thing twice more, and he responds *"Yes"* both times.

9:57am: One of the Flight 93 hijackers in the cockpit asks if anything is going on, apparently meaning outside the cockpit. *"Fighting,"* the other one says. An analysis of the flight recorder suggests that the passenger struggle actually started in the front of the plane (where Bingham and Burnett were sitting) about a minute before a struggle in the back of the plane (where Beamer was sitting). Officials later theorize that the Flight 93 passengers did actually reach the cockpit using a food cart as a battering ram and a shield. They claim that digital enhancement of the cockpit voice recorder reveals the sound of plates and glassware crashing around 9:57am. *"In the cockpit! In the cockpit!"* is heard. Hijackers are reportedly heard telling each other to hold the door. In English, someone outside shouts, *"Let's get them."* The hijackers are also praying *"Allah o akbar"* (God is great). One of the hijackers suggests shutting off the oxygen supply to the cabin (which apparently wouldn't have had an effect since the plane was already below 10,000 feet). A hijacker says, *"Should we finish?"* Another one says, *"Not yet."* The sounds of the passengers get clearer, and in unaccented English *"Give it to me!"* is heard. *"I'm injured"*, someone says in English. Then something like *"roll it up"* and *"lift it up"* is heard. Passengers' relatives believe this sequence proves that the passengers did take control of the plane.

9:58am: Confrontation with the hijackers and the passengers has begun aboard Flight 93. Emergency dispatcher Glen Cramer in Pennsylvania receives a call from a passenger on Flight 93. The passenger says: *"We are being hijacked!"*
"We confirmed that with him several times," Cramer said, *"and we asked him to repeat what he said. He was very distraught. He said he believed the plane was going down. He did hear some sort of an explosion and saw white smoke coming from the plane, but he didn't know where. And then we lost contact with him."* This was the last cell phone call made from any passengers on any of the hijacked planes.

9:58am: Todd Beamer ends his long phone call saying that they plan "to jump" the hijacker in the back who has the bomb. In the background, the phone operator already could hear an "awful commotion" of people shouting, and women screaming, *"Oh my God"*, and *"God help us."* He lets go of the phone but leaves it connected. His famous last words are said to nearby passengers: *"Are you ready guys? Let's roll."* (alternate version: *"You ready? Okay. Let's roll."*)

9:58am: CeeCee Lyles says to her husband, *"Aah, it feels like the plane's going down."* Her husband Lorne says, *"What's that?"* She replies, *"I think they're going to do it. They're forcing their way into the cockpit"* (an alternate version says, *"They're getting ready to force their way into the cockpit"*). A little later she screams, then says, *"They're doing it! They're doing it! They're doing it!"* Her husband hears more screaming in the background, then he hears a "whooshing sound, a sound like wind," then more screaming, and then the call breaks off.

9:58am: Sandy Bradshaw tells her husband, *"Everyone's running to first class. I've got to go. Bye."* She had been speaking with him since 9:50am.

NOTE: If Flight 93 passengers had taken over the plane sooner, there was at least one passenger, Don Greene, who was a professional pilot, who learned to fly at age 14, as well as Andrew Garcia, a former air traffic controller, who were both traveling on Flight 93.

9:59am: The south tower of the World Trade Center suddenly collapses, plummeting into the streets below. A massive cloud of dust and debris quickly fills lower Manhattan.

10:00am: Bill Wright is flying a small plane when an air traffic controller asks him to look around outside his window. He sees United Airlines Flight 93 three miles away - close enough to see the United Airlines colors. Air traffic control asked him the plane's altitude, then commands him to get away from the plane and land immediately. Wright saw the plane rock back and forth three or four times before he flew from the area. He speculates that the hijackers were trying to throw off the attacking passengers.

10:02am: After a review of radar tapes, a radar signal of United Airlines Flight 93 is detected near Shanksville, Pennsylvania.

10:06am: According to the FBI, the cockpit voice recorder stops and United Airlines Flight 93 crashes near Shanksville, Pennsylvania, in Somerset county, about 80 miles southeast of Pittsburgh. This is 124 miles or 15 minutes away at 500mph from Washington, D.C. An eyewitness reports seeing a white plane resembling a fighter jet circling the site just after the crash. It is now believed its target was the White House. UA Flight 93 was generally obliterated upon landing, except for one half ton piece of engine found over a mile away.

10:08am: President Bush is told of the crash of Flight 93. Because of Cheney's earlier order, he asks, *"Did we shoot it down or did it crash?"* Several hours later, he is assured it crashed.

Eyewitness accounts of United American Flight 93 crash:

Terry Butler, at Stoystown: He sees the plane come out of the clouds, low to the ground. *"It was moving like you wouldn't believe. Next thing I knew it makes a heck of a sharp, right-hand turn."* It banks to the right and appears to be trying to climb to clear one of the ridges, but it continues to turn to the right and then veers behind a ridge. About a second later it crashes.

Eric Peterson of Lambertsville: He sees a plane flying overhead unusually low. The plane seemed to be turning end-over-end as it dropped out of sight behind a tree line.

Bob Blair of Stoystown: He sees the plane spiraling and flying upside down before crashing. It's not much higher than the treetops.

Rob Kimmel, several miles from the crash site: He sees it fly overhead, banking hard to the right. It is 200 feet or less off the ground as it crests a hill to the southeast. *"I saw the top of the plane, not the bottom."*

Tim Thornsberg, working in a nearby strip mine: *"It came in low over the trees and started wobbling. Then it just rolled over and was flying upside down for a few seconds ... and then it kind of stalled and did a nose dive over the trees."* [2]

Lee Purbaugh, 300 yards away: *"There was an incredibly loud rumbling sound and there it was, right there, right above my head maybe 50 feet up... I saw it rock from side to side then, suddenly, it dipped and dived, nose first, with a huge explosion, into the ground. I knew immediately that no one could possibly have survived."*

View more eyewitness accounts of UA Flight 93 crash: **http://911research.wtc7.net/planes/evidence/eyewitness.html**

10:07am: A NYC Police helicopter sends an urgent message over the radio that the North Tower is leaning and in imminent danger of collapse.

10:08am: Secret Service agents armed with automatic rifles are deployed into Lafayette Park across from the White House.

10:10am: The FAA orders all planes to land at nearest airports.
10:10am: The FBI headquarters is evacuated.
10:10am: The Pentagon "E Section" collapses.

10:22am: In Washington, D.C., the Justice and State departments are evacuated, along with the World Bank.

10:28am: The North Tower of the World Trade Center collapses. The fact that the northern tower withstood much longer than the southern one is later attributed to three facts: the region of impact was higher, the speed of the airplane was lower, and the affected floors had their fire proofing upgraded. The World Trade Center smoldering pits of molten steel burned for exactly 100 days despite the constant spray of water being applied. The fires were finally reported extinguished on December 19.

There were 2,803 known human beings buried dead and alive when the World Trade Center Towers crumbled into 3 billion tons of debris 6 stories below the surface and 6 stories above the surface. A total of 343 firefighters, 2 paramedics, 84 Port Authority officers, 60 policemen, EMS & rescue workers, first responders who rushed into the devastation to assist traumatized evacuees to escape, were also killed. Miraculously, 23 people survived the collapse, amid steel beams, concrete slabs, and other wreckage.

All survivors had one thing in common: survivors ended up near the top of the debris. When the buildings fell, other people - no one knows just how many - also survived the immediate collapse. They were heard on fire department radios, and their bodies with no apparent fatal injuries were later found deceased, days or weeks later, almost intact, inside protective pockets deep within the tangle of steel and cement at Ground Zero. They could not be reached in time because of the immense depth of the rubble.

From this day of terror, miracles were rare, but noticed. For the 23 who survived, the difference between life and death was that they could see sunlight after the collapse, or were with someone who could. It was, in the truest sense, a ray of hope.

10:32am: Vice President Cheney calls President Bush on Air Force One, on its way from Florida to Washington, to say the White House had just received a threat against his plane. The caller had used its code word, "Angel," suggesting terrorists had inside information.

Andy Card was told it would take between 40 minutes and 90 minutes to get a protective fighter escort up to Air Force One. President Bush told an aide that Air Force One "is next." He was in an angry mood. *"We're going to find out who did this,"* he said to Cheney, *"and we're going to kick their asses."*

10:41am: Air Force One was still en route to Washington when Vice President Cheney called again. This time, he urged Bush not to return, *"There's still a threat to Washington."* Presidential National Security Advisor Condoleezza Rice agreed and had told Bush the same thing. There was little debate or discussion. Cheney was worried the terrorists might be trying to decapitate the government, to kill its leaders. Bush agreed.

10:43am: Air Force One banks suddenly and sharply to the left, its course now westerly toward Barksdale Air Force Base in Louisiana. It was within easy range, and once there, food and fuel could be loaded, and the President could have access to its more sophisticated communications systems.

10:45am: All federal office buildings in Washington, D.C. are evacuated.

10:46am: US Secretary of State Colin Powell cuts short his trip to Latin America to return to the United States.

10:50am: Five stories of the Pentagon collapse due to the fire.

10:53am: New York election primaries are postponed.

11:45am: From Barksdale Air Force Base in Louisiana, Bush made a brief and informal initial statement to the effect that terrorism on US soil would not be tolerated, stating that *"freedom itself has been attacked and freedom will be protected."*

12:36pm: President Bush appears on television from the Barksdale Air Force Base conference room. He reassures that all appropriate security measures are being taken, including putting the United States military on high alert worldwide. He also asks for prayers for those killed or wounded in the attacks and says: *"Make no mistake, the United States will hunt down and punish those responsible for these cowardly acts."*
When he got to the last sentence, he seemed to gain strength. *"The resolve of our great nation is being tested,"* he said in even tones. *"But make no mistake: We will show the world that we will pass this test."*

1:44pm: The Pentagon says five warships and two aircraft carriers (USS George Washington and USS John F. Kennedy) will leave Norfolk, Virginia, to protect the East Coast from further attack and to reduce the number of ships in port.

1:48pm: President Bush leaves Barksdale Air Force Base in Louisiana aboard Air Force One and flies to an undisclosed location. He flies to the Strategic Air Command (SAC) bunker at Offutt Air Force Base in Nebraska where there were secure facilities that would allow the president to conduct a meeting of his National Security Council in Washington over a video link.
On the plane, Bush expressed his irritation over being away from the White House. *"I want to go back home ASAP,"* he told Card, according to notes of the conversation. *"I don't want whoever did this holding me outside of Washington."*
Some aides recall Bush saying he would return to Washington later in the day, unless there was some extraordinary new threat. The senior Secret Service agent aboard Air Force One told Bush the situation was "too unsteady still" to allow his return. *"The right thing is to let the dust settle,"* Card said.

2:36pm: En route to Offutt, President Bush reached his father on the phone. His aides left him alone in the cabin. *"Where are you?"* Bush recalled asking his father. The former president said he and his wife, Barbara, were in Milwaukee, on their way to Minneapolis. *"What are you doing in Milwaukee?"* inquired the President. *"You grounded my plane,"* the former President said.

2:50pm: Before leaving Air Force One, Bush repeated to his lead Secret Service agent, *"We need to get back to Washington. We don't need some tinhorn terrorist to scare us off. The American people want to know where their president is."*

3:06pm: Air Force One landed at US Strategic Air Command at Offutt Air Force Base in Nebraska. Bush was driven the short distance to the US Strategic Command headquarters and was ushered into the secure command center, a cavernous room with multi-story video screens and batteries of military personnel at computer terminals hooked into satellites monitoring activities around the globe.

As Bush arrived, they were tracking a commercial airliner on its way from Spain to the United States. It was giving out an emergency signal, indicating it might be hijacked.

Warren Buffett, (reported to be the second richest person on Earth), was hosting a golf outing for top Corporate CEOs, at the same Offutt Air Force Base in Nebraska.

4:30pm: NORAD releases a statement that denies it had anything to do with shooting down United Airlines Flight 93.

4:36pm: The President leaves Offutt Air Force Base in Nebraska aboard Air Force One to return to Washington, D.C. Air Force One now has an F-16 guarding it, off a wing.

5:20pm: World Trade Center **Building 7**, a 47-story skyscraper, collapses. The evacuated building is damaged when the twin towers across the street collapsed earlier in the day. The CIA (secretly), and the United States Secret Service, had offices in this building. How and why World Trade Center Building 7 fell is still quite a mystery. *See Chapter 5

6:00pm: Iraq announces the attacks are the fruit of "US crimes against humanity" in an official announcement on state television.

6:54pm: President Bush arrives back at the White House aboard Marine One and is scheduled to address the nation at 8:30pm. The President landed earlier at Andrews Air Force Base with a three-fighter jet escort. *CNN*'s John King reports Laura Bush arrived earlier by motorcade from a "secure location."

7:17pm: US Attorney General John Ashcroft says the FBI is setting up a website for tips on the attacks: www.ifccfbi.gov. He also says family and friends of possible victims can leave contact information at (800) 331-0075.

8:30pm: President Bush addresses the nation again, saying, *"Thousands of lives were suddenly ended by evil."* He then asked for prayers for the families and friends of the victims. *"These acts shatter steel, but they cannot dent the steel of American resolve,"* he concluded. The President expressed that the US government will make no distinction between the terrorists who committed the acts, **and those who harbor them**. He adds that government offices in Washington are reopening for essential personnel Tuesday night, and for all workers on Wednesday.

9:00pm: President Bush met with his full National Security Council, followed roughly half an hour later by the meeting with a smaller group of key advisers who would become his war cabinet. Cheney raised the military problem of retaliating against al Qaeda's home base, noting that in Afghanistan, a country decimated by two decades of war, it would be hard to find anything to hit.
Bush returned to the problem of Osama bin Laden's sanctuary in Afghanistan. Tenet said they must deny the terrorists that sanctuary by targeting the Taliban as well. *"Tell the Taliban we're finished with them,"* he urged.
Rumsfeld said the problem was not just bin Laden and al Qaeda but the countries that supported terrorism - the point of the president's address that night. Bush said, *"We have to force countries to choose."*

9:22pm: *Fox* News reports the fire at the Pentagon is still burning and is considered contained, but not under control.

9:30pm: Bush brought together his most senior national security advisers in a bunker beneath the White House grounds. It was just 13 hours after the deadliest attack on the US homeland in the country's history. At the war cabinet, discussion turned to whether Osama bin Laden's al Qaeda network and the Taliban were the same. Tenet said they were. Osama bin Laden had bought his way into Afghanistan, supplying the Taliban with tens of millions of dollars.

11:00pm: The war cabinet finishes its meeting and has decided to embark upon a military strike against Afghanistan, and a prolonged war on terror.

11:00pm: There are reports of survivors buried in the rubble in New York making cell phone calls.

11:08pm: President Bush is at the White House. Like his father, Bush kept a daily diary of his thoughts and observations. That night, he dictated: *"The Pearl Harbor of the 21st century took place today."*

11:20pm: President Bush and his wife were awakened by Secret Service agents. The agents rushed them downstairs to the bunker because of a report of an unidentified plane in the area. The President was in running shorts and a T-shirt as he made his way down the stairs, through the tunnel and into a bunker. It proved to be a false alarm, and the Bushes returned to the residence for the rest of the night.

11:59:59pm: The United Nations International Day of Peace ends.[3]

On September 11, 2001, St. Paul's Chapel stood in the shadow of the World Trade Center Towers. Though it should have been leveled in the crashing debris of the Twin Towers, it miraculously escaped destruction in the 9/11 aftermath. St. Paul's Chapel became an on-site center for rescue efforts and a place of peaceful refuge in the midst of the chaos.

The 102 minutes between the first impact and final collapse of the North Tower allowed the vast majority of its occupants below the crash zone to escape to safety. The estimated 1,344 people above the 91st floor are believed to have not survived.

At 10:07am a police helicopter radioed a warning for firefighters to evacuate the North Tower because the South Tower had just collapsed. Unfortunately, most of the firefighters' radios did not work inside the towers, and few heard orders to evacuate. 121 FDNY firefighters were killed when the North Tower collapsed. Evacuation of the South Tower started immediately after the 8:46am jet collision with the North Tower. However, there was some confusion caused by announcements over the PA system that the building was secure and people could return to their offices. Heeding this advice perhaps cost the lives of hundreds of people.

When the UA jet hit 78-84th floors of the South Tower, it cut off most escape routes 30 floors above the impact zone. It did leave at least one of the stairwells passable, and the *New York Times* found at least 18 people who escaped through that stairwell. Most people above the crash zone were not aware of the escape route, and at least 200 climbed toward the roof in the hopes of being rescued there, only to find the doors to the roof locked.

Today, new buildings continue to rise at the World Trade Center location. Developer Larry Silverstein joined other collaborators and engineers to update construction and occupancy in the new towers. One World Trade Center, formerly known as the Freedom Tower, now stands 104 stories tall. It is the world's fifth tallest skyscraper. WTC Tower 4 reached 72 stories. Both buildings opened in 2013 and 2014. WTC Tower 3 is scheduled to open in 2018 with 80 floors. Tower 7 was completed in 2006 at 52 floors. Tower 2 is set to stair-step up 80 stories with no projected date of completion at the writing of this book.

"Today for the first time since 9/11, every part of the World Trade Center is under construction," said Silverstein. *"More than 3,000 construction workers shaped millions of tons of concrete and steel and glass into iconic buildings that will soon reclaim New York's skyline."*

View WTC and 9/11 Memorial websites:

wtc.com ~ onewtc.com ~ http://www.911memorial.org

See a birds-eye view atop One World Trade Center:

http://time.com/world-trade-center/

On September 11, patriotic Americans do not celebrate acts of terror nor radical Islamic jihad. More importantly, on this day, we exclusively and proudly celebrate the courage and heroism of 9/11 victims, who looked fear in the face of likely death, and decided to act bravely, to do what they had to do to cope with a nightmare in broad daylight.

These are the BEST of what makes America great. These are real-world heroes in these United States of America.

9/11 Fatalities:
WTC -- **2819** NYC Medical Examiner count / **2823** NYC Police count
    *NYC Firefighters -- **343**
        *Port Authority of New York and New Jersey Police -- **37**
        *NYC Police -- **23**
Pentagon -- **189** (59 flight passengers, 125 inside the Pentagon, 5 terrorists)
United Airlines Flight 93, Shanksville, Pennsylvania -- **44**
Total Fatalities – up to 3,056
Complete Listing of 9/11 Victims:
foxnews.com/story/2009/09/10/list-victims-from-sept-11-2001.html

More than 90 countries lost citizens at the World Trade Center September 11, 2001. Most of those who died were US citizens. The other countries with the highest losses are the United Kingdom (including the British overseas territory of Bermuda) with 67, the Dominican Republic with 47, and India with 41.The youngest victim was 18, and the oldest was 79.

Excluding the 19 perpetrators of the attacks, 372 foreign nationals represented more than 12% of the total number of deaths in the attacks; the majority being British, Dominican, Indian, South Korean, Canadian and Japanese.

Before the Twin Towers collapsed, an estimated 200 people jumped to their deaths from burning towers, landing on the streets and rooftops of adjacent buildings hundreds of feet below at a speed of almost 150 miles per hour - sufficient to cause instantaneous death upon impact, but insufficient to cause unconsciousness throughout the actual fall.

Most of those who fell from the World Trade Center jumped from the North Tower. To witnesses on the ground, many of the people falling from the towers seemed to have deliberately jumped to their deaths, including the person whose photograph became known as the *Falling Man*:
https://en.wikipedia.org/wiki/The_Falling_Man

A NIST report from the US Department of Commerce officially describes the deaths of 104 jumpers, but states that this figure likely understates the true number of those who had died in this manner. The sight and sound of individuals falling from the towers, then "smashing like eggs on the ground" horrified and traumatized many witnesses. The jumpers' death certificates state the cause of death as homicide due to "blunt trauma."

Some of the occupants of each tower above its point of impact made their way upward toward the roof in hope of helicopter rescue, only to find the roof access doors locked. Port Authority officers attempted to unlock the doors but control systems would not let them; in any case, thick smoke and intense heat would have prevented rescue helicopters from landing.

Cantor Fitzgerald L.P., an investment bank on the 101-105th floors of One World Trade Center, lost 658 employees, considerably more than any other employer. Marsh Inc., located immediately below Cantor Fitzgerald on floors 93-100 (the location of AA Flight 11's impact), lost 295 employees and 63 consultants. Risk Waters, a business organization, was holding a conference in Windows on the World atop North Tower One, with 81 people in attendance, all of whom perished.

As many as 600 people were killed at or above the floors of impact in the South Tower. Only 18 people are known to have managed to escape using Staircase A before the South Tower collapsed. 110 people killed in the attacks are known to have been below the impact zone when United Airlines Flight 175 struck the South Tower. The *9/11 Commission* notes that this fact strongly indicates that evacuation below the impact zones was a success, allowing most to safely evacuate before the collapse of the World Trade Center.

An additional 24 people officially remain listed as missing. This included a bomb sniffing dog named Sirius, which was not included in the official death toll.

In 2007, the New York City medical examiner's office began to add people to the official death toll who died of illnesses caused by exposure to dust from the site. The first such victim was a woman who had died in February 2002 from a lung condition. In 2009, a man was added who had died in 2008, and in 2011, a man who died in 2010.

Additionally, 1,140 responders and people who worked, lived, or studied in Lower Manhattan at the time have since been diagnosed with cancer. Over 1,400 rescue workers have died since the 9/11 attacks. Many of these were volunteers continuously responding to the scene months after the attacks.

It is also known that there were **eleven unborn babies** who died on 9/11/2001.

Dianne T. Signer was five days from her wedding in Freeport and six months away from the birth of her first child when she died in the World Trade Center's Islamic terrorist attacks on 9/11.

Louis Massari, whose wife, Patricia, 25, of Glendale, Queens, learned on the morning of 9/11/2001 that she was pregnant, told *Newsday* in 2002 that the couple had cried tears of joy before she went to work at the World Trade Center and never returned.[4]

A total of 6,294 people were reported to have been treated in area hospitals for injuries related to the New York City attacks.

Firefighters sprayed millions of gallons of water on the fires, and also applied high-tech fire retardants. Specifically, 4 million gallons of water were dropped on Ground Zero within the first 10 days after September 11, 2001.[5]

Many workers looking deep within a zigzag of underground steel girders could see a dim glow from a molten sea of burning lava. As late as five months after the attacks, in February 2002, firefighter Joe O'Toole saw a steel beam being lifted from deep underground at Ground Zero, which, he says, *"was dripping from the molten steel."* [6]

Falling Man, jumpers, trapped people:

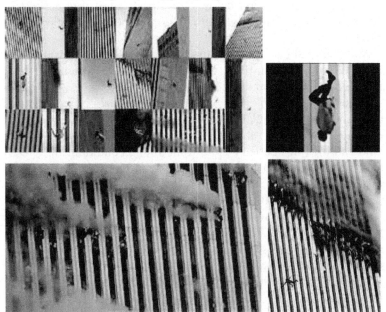

American Airlines Flight 11, WTC North Tower One:

United American Flight 175, WTC South Tower Two:

Some 18,000 people showed up to work at the WTC towers on September 11, 2001; and around 3,000 died. [7]

List of WTC tenants:
http://www.cnn.com/SPECIALS/2001/trade.center/tenants1.html

United American Flight 93, Shanksville, PA:

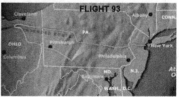

American Airlines Flight 77, US Pentagon:

 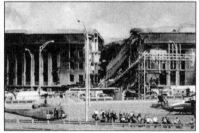

(4) Flights map:

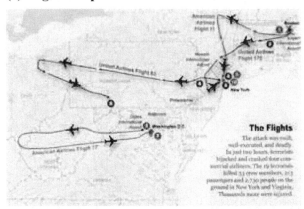

World Trade Center on 9/11/2001:

Chapter Three

9/11 Survivors

The attacks of September 11th were intended to break our spirit. Instead, we have emerged stronger and more unified. We feel renewed devotion to the principles of political, economic and religious freedom, the rule of law and respect for human life. We are more determined than ever to live our lives in freedom.[1]

Rudolph W. Giuliani, December 31, 2001

New York City Mayor, 1994-2001

Firefighters and rescue workers endured 2,000°F heat waves belching upwards from the heart of tangled vines of molten steel. The rescue efforts were extremely dangerous, putting hundreds of volunteers' lives at immediate risk. As mentioned in the previous chapter, many working to save others suffered permanent injury themselves, even death, weeks and months thereafter due to illnesses caused by exposure to dust from Ground Zero.

Because American pride seeks a measure of victory even in defeat, twenty-three people total were miraculously pulled out alive from the rubble of the Twin Towers, including 15 rescue workers. The last survivor to be removed alive from the debris was from the ruins of the North Tower 27 hours after its collapse.

Among the most notable rescuers is David Karnes. An ex-Marine, Karnes was working as an accountant in Wilton, CT, when he witnessed the planes crashing into the WTC Towers LIVE on TV. Karnes said to his co-workers, *"You guys may not realize it, but this country is at war."* [2]

Karnes drove immediately to a local church and asked the pastor and parishioners to say a prayer that God would lead him to survivors. A devout Christian, Karnes often turned to prayer when faced with real-world, tough decisions.

Karnes got a regulation military-style hair cut, put on his Marine Corps camouflage utility uniform and gathered equipment that included rappelling gear, ropes, canteens of water, his Marine Corps K-Bar knife, and a flashlight. He drove from Connecticut to the World Trade Center the following morning at speeds of up to 120 mph to assist with disaster relief.

Karnes rode into the WTC debris site with his Porsche convertible down, so that security personnel could see his military uniform and wave him through. Once inside, he met Marine Sgt. Jason Thomas shortly thereafter, who had also been searching for survivors.

They climbed over the tangled steel and began looking into voids. They saw no one else searching the pile, because rescue workers previously obeyed an order to leave the area, as it was too dangerous to stand upon. Yet, they climbed the mountain of debris, skirting dangerous crevasses and shards of red-hot metal, calling out, *"United States Marines! Is anyone down there? If you can hear us, yell or tap!"* [3]

Over and over, Karnes shouted the words. Then he would pause and listen. Debris was shifting and parts of the building were collapsing further. Fires burned all around. *"I just had a sense, an overwhelming sense, come over me that we were walking on hallowed ground, that tens of thousands of people could be trapped and dead beneath us,"* Karnes reflects. [4]

Karnes recalls he saw children's shoes, Raggedy Ann dolls and women's heels as he navigated the flaming debris. He could smell the hair and flesh from hundreds of burning bodies.

After about an hour of searching and yelling, Karnes stopped. *"Be quiet,"* he told Thomas, *"I think I can hear something."*

He yelled again. *"We can hear you. Yell louder."* He heard a faint muffled sound in the distance. *"Keep yelling. We can hear you."* Karnes and Thomas zeroed in on the sound. [5]

"We're over here," they heard. The two men found Will Jimeno and John McLoughlin, a pair of police officers buried in the rubble around a freight elevator for about 13 and 22 hours. McLoughlin was buried deeper in the rubble, which took a lengthier rescue effort.

Karnes called his sister and had her patch him through to the New York Police Department. A paramedic showed up first, and he and Karnes began lifesaving measures. The first rescue took 3.5 hours, and the second took seven hours. [6]

Karnes spent a total of nine days at the site before returning to his office in CT. Upon returning home, he reenlisted in the Marine Corps Reserve and went on to serve in the Philippines and Iraq. He served for 17 months, including two tours of duty in Iraq.

Karnes is portrayed by actor Michael Shannon in the 2006 Oliver Stone feature film *World Trade Center*. Will Jimeno was played by actor Michael Peña, and John McLoughlin by actor Nicholas Cage.

Karnes did not participate in the making of Stone's *World Trade Center* movie due to Stone's anti-Bush views. Karnes says Oliver Stone took a lot of liberties with the actual events of that day. Rebecca Liss of *Slate* magazine observed, *"The film seems to overplay his zeal without conveying his motivations and reasoning. He [Karnes] is unfairly portrayed as a robotic soldier of Christ—a little wacky and simplistic."* [7]

Though he does not seek the limelight of fame, nor heroism, David Karnes is regarded by most sensible, patriotic Americans as a hero of 9/11.

Marine Sergeant Jason Thomas was portrayed in Oliver Stone's *World Trade Center* by white actor William Mapother. Stone has said he was not aware that Thomas was black until filming was already underway.

On February 11, 2007, *Extreme Makeover: Home Edition* aired a special two-hour episode about Thomas and his family. Following the attacks, Thomas and his wife had moved their four children from New York to Whitehall, Ohio. The house they bought began to deteriorate and the show intervened to help them be able to live in a brand new home.

9/11 is the title of a 2002 French-American documentary film by brothers Jules and Gedeon Naudet originally filming Tony Benetatos, a "newbie" firefighter on the New York City Fire Department assigned to the Engine 7/Ladder 1/Battalion 1 Firehouse on Duane Street in Lower Manhattan. The original intention of the film was to chronicle the rookie's first experiences as a firefighter.

On the morning of September 11, 2001, the firehouse, under the direction of Battalion Chief Joseph Pfeifer, was called out on a reported "odor of gas" at Church and Lispenard Streets. Jules rode with Pfeifer to investigate, while Gedeon stayed behind at the firehouse filming the day-to-day duties of the rookie, Benetatos.

As the Battalion 1 firefighters examined the supposed gas leak, American Airlines Flight 11 flew overhead. Turning the camera to follow the plane, Jules taped one of only three known recordings of the first plane hitting the North Tower (Tower 1) of the World Trade Center.

The firefighters, under the direction of Chief Pfeifer, were the first responders on the scene, and Jules was allowed to follow and film the chief in real-time during the attempted rescue operations. Jules, Chief Pfeifer and several other FDNY Chiefs were inside the lobby of Tower 1 when Tower 2 was hit by the second aircraft and when Tower 2 eventually collapsed.

The film gives various firemen's accounts of the events of the remainder of the day - from the initial crash to the building's collapse to the attempts to rescue survivors from the rubble - as well as the aftermath of the events and those who were lost, including Chief Pfeifer's brother, Engine 33 Lieutenant Kevin Pfeifer.

The author has viewed the *9/11* film and found it to be a surreal "birds-eye account" of actual 9/11 events *as they are happening*. It shows the NY City Fire Chief making critical decisions in real-time, coupled with eerie *ka-booms!* of people purposely falling to their deaths who jumped from high upper levels of the Twin Towers due to extreme heat forcing them out.

In February 2001, Sujo John and his wife Mary moved from India and started their new life in America. They were expecting their first child and lived outside of New York City. Both of them had good jobs at the World Trade Center. Sujo worked on the 81st floor of Tower 1 (North Tower), Mary worked on the 71st floor of Tower 2 (South Tower).

On the morning of September 11, 2001, at about 8:45am, Sujo John heard a loud explosion and the building rattled and shook. People on his floor started to scream.

American Airlines Flight 11 from Boston to Los Angeles had just crashed into the building. Debris from the plane flew into the office and everything started going up in flames. Everyone in the office tried their best to stay calm. Around them there was twisted steel, smoke, and fire quickly spreading. Sujo's thoughts shifted to Tower Two where Mary was. He wondered if the plane hit her building too.

Sujo and others in the building made their way to the stairwell through debris on fire. As he was coming down the flights of stairs, he tried to call his wife on his cell phone. Unfortunately, cell phones were not working. He stopped at the 53rd floor desperately trying to make some calls from the land line, which were unsuccessful. He continued his descent from Tower One and saw hundreds of policemen and firemen passing him and others making their way up in the crowded stairwell.

Once outside, Sujo decided to make his way to Tower Two to look for Mary.

As he approached the building, there was a massive explosion and the ground around him was shaking. All 110 stories of Tower Two collapsed, as Sujo was standing near the foot of the building. The debris of the building was falling all around. Sujo and the people around him huddled together at one end of the building. He prayed for protection under the blood of Jesus and asked God to give him His strength.

Sujo felt challenged to tell the people around him that they were going to die and if anyone didn't know Jesus that they should call on His name. Then, everyone around him started crying, *"Jesus!"* The whole building collapsed as they were engulfed in debris.

Sujo found himself in three feet of white soot and glass, but no debris fell on him. When he got to his feet, it was silent and he saw dead bodies all around him.

Sujo was still worried about his wife in the other building. He continued to try to call Mary, but his cell phone still didn't work. Finally, his cell phone rang. It was Mary telling Sujo that she was alive. Apparently, Mary had not made it to work because her train arrived at the World Trade Center subway stop five minutes after the first crash and passengers were not allowed into the buildings. Mary was hysterical walking on the streets worrying about Sujo and thinking he was dead.

They each made it to 39th Street near the ferry. They looked back and saw the remains of their buildings, which were piles of smoking rubble and ashes. Throughout the tragic day's events Sujo and Mary prayed that the other would survive and fully dedicated their lives to God if they survived.

Sujo and Mary kept their promise to God. Their lives are dedicated to share their testimony of surviving 9/11 and sharing the Gospel full-time. As an evangelist, Sujo has travelled to churches all across America and other nations to minister in different churches weekly. He has a special place in his heart for India, where he travels at least four times a year.

See Sujo John's ministry: **sujojohn.com**.

One of the kindest 9/11 survivors the author encountered is the impressive Manuel Chea.

In an amazing video recording of Chea's 9/11 testimony (shown during a 2011 10th year commemoration 9/11event hosted by the author and author's father at the Lexington Civic Center in NC), Chea describes how he narrowly escaped out of the World Trade Center North Tower, and the aftereffects of that event in his own life.

Chea was working as a systems administrator on the 49th floor when he felt the plane's impact hit the 95th floor. While employees collectively helped one another to leave, Chea scrambled through hallways and down a flight of stairs as the building groaned and swayed to make it outside, as the South Tower came crashing down. Chea credits his safety to a second chance that God gave to him.

Chea now enjoys working directly with rescue responders for New York City's Emergency Management Department. Graciously volunteering to speak in schools since 2004 about 9/11, Chea's focus brings to light positive transformations in people's lives who were directly impacted by 9/11, rather than focusing only on the suffering aspect and the tragedy of 9/11.

I share my story not to focus on the dark times of 9/11,
but to focus on the hope and the strength
that faith in Jesus can bring in the face of trials.
I want to share with everyone that it is not always a big event
such as 9/11 that can overwhelm you. The worries of daily life,
work, home, and all kinds of stress can weigh heavily on anyone.
Yet as we are reminded in Isaiah 40:28-31 that God does not grow
weary or faint and that He Himself will give power to the faint and
to him who has no might he increases strength. [8]

Manuel Chea
9/11/2001 Survivor, WTC North Tower, 49th Floor

Brian Clark is a Canadian survivor of the attacks on the World Trade Center. Clark was one of only fourteen people in the South Tower to escape from a floor above the plane's impact, escaping from his office on the 84th floor. No one escaped above the impact point in the North Tower. Clark's testimony before the 9/11 Commission, where he detailed problems with the 911 emergency call system, has been widely quoted.

As Clark descended a flight of stairs, he heard a faint scream for help on the 81st floor. Clark grabbed coworker Ron DiFrancesco and entered the 81st floor to look for the person screaming for help. As Clark and DiFrancesco entered the floor, they were engulfed in smoke. DiFrancesco became overcome with smoke and returned to the stairs.

Clark, who later described a mysterious "bubble of fresh air" around him which allowed him to continue the search, made his way to find Fuji Bank employee Stanley Praimnath, who was pinned underneath some debris behind a wall.

DiFrancesco rushed down nearly 80 flights of stairs while struggling for oxygen, only to be hit by a fireball from the building's collapse. When he woke in the hospital, he had a broken back, lacerations to his head, and burns all over his body, but he miraculously survived.

All 3 made it out alive, dodging falling debris, and suffering extensive burns and head lacerations.

For others like Michael Moy, a software engineer for IQ Financial Inc., a decision to defy orders proved lifesaving. Moy was at his workstation on the 83rd floor of WTC [South] Tower Two getting ready to write software when the first jetliner struck [North]Tower One. A few minutes later, he says, building security came on the speaker and instructed occupants to remain in their offices, saying that it would be more dangerous in the streets due to falling debris from the other building.

Disobeying those instructions, Moy and his boss told the 15 or so employees in their wing to start heading down the stairs. Once again an announcement came over the speaker system, instructing employees to return to their respective floors. A few employees decided to do so and headed toward the lobby's elevators.

Just then, the doors of several elevators exploded, apparently because the second hijacked airplane had slammed into the building just a few floors above them.

Pandemonium followed. Being familiar with the stairway systems in the building, Moy and his boss directed co-workers to a little-used stairway that was relatively empty. As a result, dozens of people were able to hurry downstairs and escape into the street. *"I'm glad we acted the way we did,"* says Moy. [9]

Tom Canavan, who worked for First Union Bank, stayed on the 47th floor of the North Tower until after the South Tower was hit. Then, Canavan descended the stairs and passed through revolving doors into the darkened, glass-strewn underground shopping mall between the two Towers, and had turned back to help a couple, when the rumble of the South Tower's destruction began.

He was thrown to the ground and trapped in a small space by slabs of concrete.

Canavan and another man crawled to an opening near "The Sphere" -- the World Trade Center Plaza's centerpiece bronze sculpture. The other man crawled out, but Canavan, being larger, was unable to.

Canavan continued to struggle, and crawled 40 feet east and 30 feet up through the rubble in 25 minutes, escaping just a few minutes before the fall of the North Tower. Canavan extracted himself and walked to safety over smoldering rubble that burned the bottoms of his shoes.

To date, the identity of the other survivor described by Canavan remains unknown.

Pasquale Buzzelli's story of 9/11 survival is extremely rare and little known. Because he lost 14 colleagues who perished on 9/11, Buzzelli did not share his story until years later due to "survivor's guilt". Buzzelli is known as the man who "surfed" down several floors of stairs to safety.

The structural engineer, age 44, was in a lift when the first plane hit the North Tower above him at the 93rd floor. He phoned his 7-month pregnant wife to find out what was going on. Climbing back inside, he watched a 2nd plane hit the adjacent South Tower on TV and immediately began to escape the building.

When he reached the 22nd floor, the North Tower building began to collapse. His wife thought her husband was dead. Buzzelli began to free fall and "bounced around" on air, like riding a roller coaster as he describes it, until he experienced a bright flash of light, then fell unconscious.

Buzzelli awoke three hours later, lying on a ledge of the ruins seven floors up. Despite falling 15 floors, he had only suffered a broken leg and a crushed ankle. [10]

Documentary-makers met the firemen who rescued him, and scientists and engineers who said the account was plausible. Professor Thomas Eagar, from the Massachusetts Institute of Technology, said the winds from the falling towers were strong enough to lift a man into the air. [11]

Firefighters Mike Lyons and Mike Moribito, who "disobeyed" orders to search the wreckage, found Buzzelli just when he was in danger of being burnt alive.

Eighty-two percent of Lauren Manning's body was severely burned on the morning of September 11, 2001.

While headed to her job as a managing director at Cantor Fitzgerald on the 106th floor of the North Tower, she got only as far as the lobby when the elevator exploded, Lauren wrote in her book: *Love, Greg and Lauren,*

With an enormous, screeching exhalation, the fire explodes
from the elevator banks into the lobby and engulfs me,
its tentacles of flame hungrily latching on.
An immense weight pushes down on me, and I can barely breathe.
I am whipped around ... I see people lying on the floor
covered in flames, burning alive.
Like them, I am on fire. [12]

In excruciating pain, Lauren prayed for death. Then thoughts of her 10 month old son, Tyler, lent new resolve. Deciding she had not yet spent enough time with Tyler, Lauren stumbled in the streets where a heroic man ripped off his jacket to smother out flames engulfing her. Lauren knows who he is, though he has never been publicly identified: a bond trader and father of two who has "never wanted the recognition."

After one month in a coma, and six months undergoing more than 25 operational skin grafts, and the amputation of four fingertips, Lauren had to relearn to stand and walk.

Lauren is a true fighter in the American spirit. In 2004, she was chosen to participate in the International Olympic Torch Relay running three blocks in Manhattan to the cheer of onlookers and supporters.

In 2004, Lauren was named Glamour magazine's Woman of the Year.

My survival had given me a chance to make things right, to see beyond the small sorrows of everyday life. [13]

Lauren Manning
9/11/2001 WTC Survivor

Fourteen people, mostly firefighters from Ladder Company 6 and Engine 39, survived in the B stairwell of the North Tower and crawled to safety. They are firefighters Billy Butler, Tommy Falco, Jay Jonas, Michael Meldrum, Sal D'Agastino, and Matt Komorowski of Ladder 6; firefighter Mickey Kross of Engine Company 16; firefighters Jim McGlynn, Rob Bacon, Jeff Coniglio, and Jim Efthimiaddes of Engine 39; Port Authority Police Officer Dave Lim; Battalion Chief Rich Picciotto of the 11th Battalion; and civilian Josephine Harris.

Jay Jonas and other survivors waited three hours before crossing a three-story-deep trench of tangled metal to reach safety.

William Rodriguez was an American Building Maintenance employee for twenty years, responsible for inspection and maintenance at the World Trade Center. He held the master key for the stairs. He was the last person to leave the building on September 11, 2001, and has been credited with saving many lives.

Many national 9/11 organizations and survivors doubt whether Rodriguez's heroism is factual. A tart level of distrust stems from open associations with the late Venezuelan dictator Hugo Chavez.

For his efforts, Rodriguez received the National Hero Award from the Senate of Puerto Rico. Rodriguez founded the Hispanic Victims Group, Inc., in 2002. The group was one of the key forces behind the creation of the 9/11 Commission.

After a national disaster, there will inevitably be some people who pretend to be victims. They usually do it for money, which means getting access to donated relief funds.

Patriotic Americans are typically not wealthy snobs, but are grassroots, generous citizens, who see suffering and take action to "pitch in" and help the unfortunate, sometimes sacrificing their own finances to do so.

Unfortunately, *they* sometimes become victims of fraud.

Another segment of society seeks to plunder private or business property amidst the chaos of disaster to steal goods. While first responders and law officers are handling victims, or the crisis itself, thieves are plundering elsewhere.

From September 2001-2007, the Manhattan District Attorney's Office handed down 539 charges of crimes related to the regional collapse at the World Trade Center. Trespassing, shoplifting, breaking and entering, as well as fraud, topped the list of offenses.

People claimed to have lost jobs they didn't have, or claimed to lose a spouse they didn't lose. Many tried to get a "slice of pie" from the Victim Compensation Fund. In all, 76% of the charges resulted in convictions.

Some perpetrators didn't desire money, just a crazy thirst for attention. Example: Sugeil Mejia frantically told police two days after the 9/11 attacks that her husband was trapped in a pile of rubble and called her on his cell phone. Police raced her to Ground Zero, putting rescue worker's lives at risk searching in the shifting, unstable rubble. Sugeil vanished shortly thereafter with her two kids. Four months later, Sugeil pleaded guilty in Manhattan Superior Court and served a 3 year prison sentence for reckless endangerment.

Tania Head was not even her real name. Alicia Esteve Head came from a wealthy Spanish family, and on Sept. 11, 2001, she had been in graduate school in Barcelona. She arrived in the US in 2003.

"Tania" Head contacted 9/11 survivor, Gerry Bogacz, member of the 9/11 Survivors Network (**survivorsnet.org**) Sharing email conversations for 2 months, they swapped 9/11 survivor stories with one another. Only problem is, Tania Head was a 9/11 faker.

Her bogus 9/11 story was a sorted tale of being badly burned when the hijacker plane crashed into the 78th floor of the South Tower, while working for Merrill Lynch. She claimed to have encountered a dying man who gave her his wedding band, which she also claimed to have returned to his wife weeks later. Head claims her husband, Dave, perished in the North Tower crash. Head became a spokesperson, and later..would you believe, President, of the 9/11 Survivors Network. She escorted dignitaries and concerned citizens on several tours through the Ground Zero rebuilding projects. She delivered heart-felt speeches to college groups, religious organizations, and victim groups, who swooned at her stories of 9/11 survival. No one questioned Head's authenticity probably due to the gripping immediacy and pain of her account.

It wasn't until 5 years later that details of her story were fact-checked by major news outlets and questions were raised. Her original story of 9/11 survival didn't add up. Not one person Head claimed to have encountered, helped, or met on Sept. 11, 2001, had any recollection of her.

The husband Head claimed died in the North Tower had family who had never seen, met, nor heard of her. Merrill Lynch has no record, nor paycheck stubs, of her employment. Head had told people that she earned an undergraduate degree from Harvard and a graduate business degree from Stanford, though officials at both universities said they could not find records of a student by her name.

Head said she established a foundation in memory of her late husband, *Dave's Children Foundation*, and has served as its executive director. But there are no registration records of such a charity on file neither with the federal government nor with the state of New York.

Head began to decline several interviews citing pangs of "private and emotional turmoil".

The board of the 9/11 Survivors Network voted in 2012 to remove her as President of the group. Officials of the Tribute Center stopped Head from doing volunteer work as a tour guide. *"At this time, we are unable to confirm the veracity of her connection to the events of Sept. 11,"* said Jennifer Adams, chief executive of the September 11th Families Association, which developed the center.[14]

Head melded back into society but apparently resurfaced years later at a White Plains, NY, memorial; this time in the role of Ester DiNardo, a supposed victim's mother.

See the 9/11 Survivors Network online: **survivorsnet.org.**

Ground Zero, New York City:

David Karnes:

Michael Shannon

Jason Thomas:

Sujo and Mary John:

Stanley Praimnath & Brian Clark:

Pasquale Buzzelli:

Lauren Manning:

Stairwells of the WTC Twin Towers on 9/11/2001:

Credit: Shannon Stapleton-Files, Reuters

William Rodriguez:

Tania Head (Alicia Esteve Head):

Will Jimeno and John McLoughlin:

Miscellaneous photos, Ground Zero:

Chapter Four

9/11 History

We Will Remember - September 11, 2001

Car Window Decal

September 11, 0009. The Battle of the Teutoburg Forest ends. An alliance of Germanic tribes led by Arminius ambushed and decisively destroyed three Roman legions and their auxiliaries, led by Publius Quinctilius Varus. The Roman Army never again attempted to conquer Germanian territory east of the Rhine River. Modern historians have regarded Arminius' victory as "Rome's greatest defeat" and one of the most decisive battles in history.

September 11, 813. Charles the Great (Charlemagne, King of the Franks) crowns Louis I Roman Emperor of modern day France and Germany, called the Carolingian Empire.

September 11, 1297. In the First War of Scottish Independence, Scottish rebel William Wallace defeats the English at the Battle of Stirling Bridge.

September 11, 1565. The Knights of Malta led by a 70 year old Frenchmen, Jean Parisot de la Valette, defended the Republic of Malta, an island in the Mediterranean Sea from Sultan Suleiman the Magnificent, and Algerian Admiral Dragut with his 200 ships and 40,000 Muslim soldiers. Had the Muslim marauders won, Spain and Italy would be living under the Koran.

September 11, 1683. Sultan Mehmed IV sent over 138,000 Muslim Ottoman Turks to surround Vienna, Austria, led by General Mustafa Pasha. For two months they had starved the 11,000 Hapsburg-Austrian defenders. Mehmed IV sent the message to Austrian King, Leopold I:

"Await us in your residence...so we can decapitate you." [1]

Polish King Jan Sobieski gathered 81,000 Polish, Austrian and German troops and on September 11, 1683, led a surprise attack. In one of the largest charges in history; 38,350 cavalry and dragoon guards, with many wearing wings which made a thunderous sound, caused the Turks to flee in confusion.

The Pope and European leaders hailed Jan Sobieski as the "Savior of Western Civilization." The humiliated Muslim army beheaded General Mustafa Pasha and sent his head back to Sultan Mehmed IV in a velvet bag.

Hilaire Belloc (1870-1953) wrote in *The Great Heresies* (1938):

*Less than 100 years before the American War of Independence a
Mohammedan army was threatening to overrun and destroy
Christian civilization. Vienna was almost taken and only saved by
the Christian army under the command of the King of Poland on a
date that ought to be among the most famous in history -
September 11, 1683.* [2]

*NOTE: Get the book, **"What Every American Needs to Know
about the Qur`an: A History of Islam and the United States"** by
William J. Federer:
amazon.com/Every-American-Needs-about-Quran/dp/0977808556

September 11, 1697. Habsburg Prince Eugene of Savoy led the
Holy League to counter-attack Muslim Ottoman Turks against
their siege of Belgrade, Serbia. Losing 500 men, they killed 30,000
Turks in one of the Ottoman Empire's worst defeats in history - the
Battle of Zenta, September 11, 1697. This ended Ottoman (Turkish
Muslim) control of large parts of Central Europe.

September 11, 1708. Charles XII of Sweden stops his march to
conquer Moscow outside Smolensk, marking the turning point in
the Great Northern War. The army is defeated nine months later in
the Battle of Poltava, and the Swedish empire is no longer a major
European power.

September 11, 1776. A British–American peace conference on
Staten Island fails to stop a nascent American Revolutionary War.
Known as the "Staten Island Peace Conference", representatives of
the 2nd Continental Congress; Ben Franklin, John Adams, and
Edward Rutledge; met with British Admiral Lord Richard Howe.
The brief meeting took place for three hours without Admiral
Howe being unable to recognize the declared independence of the
new American states. The American Revolutionary War of 1776
began 4 days later with British occupation in New York.

September 11, 1777. The US Continental Congress was forced to evacuate Philadelphia as the British won the Battle of Brandywine, forcing General Washington and his 10,000 troops to retreat. Due to the interruption of trade, Congress was made aware of a shortage of Bibles. Congress voted shortly thereafter to import Bibles from Scotland or Ireland into the Union stating, *"The use of the Bible is so universal and its support so great, it is resolved accordingly to import said 20,000 copies of the Bible."* [3]

September 11, 1789. Alexander Hamilton is appointed the first United States Secretary of the Treasury.

September 11, 1814. Begun on September 6, Americans defeat the British at the Battle of Plattsburgh during the War of 1812, a major American victory that kept British forces from invading Washington, D.C.

September 11, 1857. In the Mountain Meadows Massacre, Mormons dressed as Indians murdered 120 colonists in Utah.

September 11, 1893. First conference of the World Parliament of Religions is held.

September 11, 1903. The first race at The Milwaukee Mile in West Allis, Wisconsin, is held. It is the oldest major speedway in the world.

September 11, 1922. One of the things that the League of Nations did during its short period of existence was to grant Great Britain a special "mandate" to establish a homeland for the Jewish people in the territory of Palestine, which had been taken from the newly defeated Turkish Empire. History records that the administration of this mandate effectively began with the swearing into office as High Commissioner and Commander in Chief for Palestine of the Right Honorable Sir Herbert Samuel, in Jerusalem, on September 11, 1922.

September 11, 1922. The final achievement of Zionism (establishment of Jewish homeland) in the post WWI period was the passage by Congress on September 11, 1922 of a joint resolution favoring a Jewish homeland in Palestine. The words of the resolution practically echoed the Balfour Declaration.

September 11, 1924. Tom Landry, American football player and coach was born. As coach of the Dallas Cowboys, Landry won two Super Bowls in 1972 and 1978. Landry is the 3rd winningest NFL coach of all time, the longest winning NFL head coach with 20 consecutive winning seasons, and the longest serving NFL head coach of one team at 29 years with the Dallas Cowboys.

September 11, 1928. W2XB (owned by General Electric's WGY) in Schenectady, NY, televised the first TV Drama program in the United States, "The Queen's Messenger," by J. Harley Manners, a blood and thunder play with guns, daggers, and poison. Technical limitations were so great and viewing screens so small, that only the actor's individual hands or faces could be seen at one time. Three cameras were used, two for the characters and a third for obtaining images of gestures and appropriate stage props.

September 11, 1928. Ty Cobb's last hitting appearance, pops out against the NY Yankees.

September 11, 1936. FDR dedicates Boulder Dam, now known as the Hoover Dam.

September 11, 1939. World War II: Canada declares war on Germany, the country's first independent declaration of war.

September 11, 1940. George Stibitz of Bell Labs pioneers the first remote operation of a digital computer. Stibitz used a "teletype" to send commands to the Complex Number Computer in New York over telegraph lines.

September 11, 1941. Construction begins on the US Pentagon.

September 11, 1941. Charles Lindbergh spoke about Jewish power in the media and government. The shy 39-year-old, known around the world for his epic 1927 New York to Paris flight, the first solo trans-Atlantic crossing, was addressing 7,000 people in Des Moines, Iowa, on September 11, 1941, about the dangers of US involvement in the war then raging in Europe. The three most important groups pressing America into war, he explained, were the British, the Jews and the Roosevelt Administration.

September 11, 1944. World War II: The first Allied troops of the US Army cross the western border of Germany.

September 11, 1945. Physician Willem J. Kolff performs the first successful kidney dialysis using his artificial kidney machine in the Netherlands.

September 11, 1946. First mobile long-distance car-to-car telephone conversation is completed. Alton Dickieson and D. Mitchell from Bell Labs, along with future AT&T CEO H.I. Romnes, were part of a team that worked more than a decade to create what they termed a "primitive wireless network" capable of transmitting phone calls. It was much less than "mobile," as the required equipment weighed in at 80 pounds.

September 11, 1950. The Dick Tracy TV show sparks a national uproar concerning violence.

September 11, 1951. Florence Chadwick becomes the first woman to swim the English Channel from England to France. It took 16 hours and 19 minutes.

September 11, 1959. The US Congress passes a bill authorizing food stamps for poor Americans.

September 11, 1967. Harry Connick, Jr., American singer-songwriter, pianist, and actor was born.

September 11, 1970. The Ford Pinto car is introduced.

September 11, 1973. President Salvador Allende of Chile was assassinated and his country taken over by a US backed coup.

September 11, 1985. Pete Rose of Cincinnati Reds gets career hit 4,192 off San Diego Padres pitcher Eric Show, eclipsing Ty Cobb's long-held MLB most hits record.

September 11, 1986. The Dow Jones Industrial Average suffered the biggest 1-day decline ever, plummeting 86.61 points to 1,792.89. There were 237.57 million shares traded.

September 11, 1994. A lone pilot crashed a stolen single-engine Cessna into a tree on the White House grounds just short of President Clinton's bedroom.

September 11, 2002. Johnny Unitas, NFL Hall of Fame football legend and sportscaster dies.

September 11, 2007. Russia tests the largest conventional weapon ever, the "Father of All Bombs."

September 11, 2009. Islamic inmates at Iraq's Abu Ghraib prison start a fire and clash with guards during two days of unrest.

September 11, 2010. The Medal of Honor is awarded for the first time since the Vietnam War. US Army Staff Sergeant Salvatore Giunta received the medal for his actions during the War in Afghanistan.

September 11, 2011. A 10th Year Commemoration of 9/11/2001 honoring all victims and first responders was held at the 1,200 seat Lexington Civic Center, Lexington, NC. The event was hosted twice in the same day (morning event and evening event) by Evangelist Jimmie M. Clark, with Dr. Troy Clark as the event organizer. Among honored guests were Manuel Chea, a 9/11 survivor who escaped out the North Tower before it collapsed, attending the event by video, a letter from President George W. Bush, and several NC Senators, Representatives, Judges, County Commissioners, City Councilmen, and Lexington, NC, Mayor.

September 11, 2012. The US Embassy in Benghazi, Libya, is attacked by Islamic militants, resulting in four American deaths. For the first time since 2001, no special security alert is issued by the US Government (under President Obama) on the anniversary of the 9/11 attacks.

Islamic militants attacked an American diplomatic consulate in Benghazi, Libya, murdering US Ambassador J. Christopher Stevens and US Foreign Service Information Management Officer Sean Smith. Several hours later, a second assault targeted a different compound about one mile away, killing two Navy SEAL CIA contractors, Tyrone S. Woods and Glen Doherty. Ten others were also injured in the attacks. The attackers were armed with assault rifles, rocket-propelled grenades, and mortars.

As aftermath facts of the Benghazi attacks surfaced, Obama's State Department officials were criticized for denying over 600 requests from Ambassador Stevens and Benghazi embassy officials for additional security at the consulate weeks prior to the attack.[4]

Secretary of State Hillary Clinton, architect of the Benghazi foreign policy failure, who was called before US Senate Hearings 5/8/2013 and 10/22/2015, also failed to satisfy ultimate responsibility for security lapses and the tortuous deaths of 4 Americans, blaming the attack on an obscure *YouTube* video that allegedly angered the Islamic attackers into a frenzied mob, while claiming none of the 600 requests for additional security ever reached her email Inbox.

Clinton, annoyed by the first hearing, screeched, *"What difference at this point does it make?!"* In the latter hearing, it was proven Clinton knew she was lying to families of the deceased, as well as media press, while explaining the cause of the attacks was an inconsequential YouTube video. Clinton inconceivably emerged from both hearings politically unscathed, while simultaneously running as a Democrat candidate for US President.

A longtime Clinton confidant reportedly advised then-Secretary of State Hillary Clinton two days after the Islamic terrorist attack that an al Qaeda-tied group had planned the deadly assault and used a public protest as a cover. Despite this warning, Clinton's U.N. ambassador went on to publicly claim the attack was "spontaneous." The incrimination from ex-Clinton aide Sidney Blumenthal was contained in a memo sent Sept. 13, 2012, according to *The New York Times*.

A Defense Intelligence Agency report from Sept. 12, 2012, marked indicators that the attack was **planned** and meant as retaliation for a previous drone strike that killed an al Qaeda strategist.

The memo, obtained through a federal lawsuit by conservative watchdog *Judicial Watch*, said: *"The attack was planned ten or more days prior to approximately 01 September 2012. The intention was to attack the consulate and to kill as many Americans as possible to seek revenge for the US killing of Aboyahiye (Alaliby) in Pakistan and in memorial of the 11 September 2001 attacks on the World Trade Center buildings."* [5]

Additional memos surfaced indicating Susan Rice, current National Security Adviser, was prepped to mislead the Sept. 16, 2012, Sunday TV news show inquiries. One email from a top administration adviser specifically drew purposeful misdirection to the obscure *YouTube* video. The email listed the following goal, among others: *"To underscore that these protests are rooted in an Internet video, and not a broader failure of policy."* [6]

Under Obama's Justice Department, no justice has ultimately been served on the perpetrators of the Islamic terrorist attack, even though we know who and where they are. Libya militia leader Ahmed Abu Khattala was captured in south Benghazi June 2014 by US commandos of the Army's Delta Force and brought to Washington, D.C. by decision of then-US Attorney General Eric Holder to be tried in a civilian court, rather than a military tribunal at Guantanamo Bay, Cuba. Critics have rightfully denounced Holder's decision, as it has mired down the progress of the case so unnecessarily slow. Holder turned the case over to District of Columbia prosecutor, Ronald C. Machen Jr., a like-minded black attorney, which is perceived to have a lower standing in the Justice Department's hierarchy than the Brooklyn, Manhattan and Northern Virginia offices, who normally handle this type of high-profile case.

The Obama administration insists it is still "trying" to apprehend another suspect, Muhammad Jamal, wanted for his role in the 2012 Islamic terrorist attack at the Benghazi embassy. Jamal was labeled a designated terrorist by the United Nations Oct. 18, 2013, identifying him and the group he formed in 2011, the Muhammad Jamal Network, as linked to the Sept. 11, 2012, Benghazi attack. He was trained as an explosives expert by al Qaeda in Afghanistan during the late 1980s, and is a former senior military commander of the Egyptian Islamic Jihad group.

Jamal has a Yemeni wife and holds a Yemeni passport. US and Egyptian authorities recently contacted the Sanaa government seeking information about him, according to a Yemeni newspaper report. Unidentified Yemeni security sources disclosed to the Aden-based *Al Umana* newspaper Dec. 2013 that U.S. intelligence agencies intercepted communications between Jamal and al Qaeda leader Ayman al Zawahiri. Jamal is **not** listed on the FBI website as one of the most wanted terrorists or among suspects listed on the FBI's "seeking terror information" page.[7]

Jamal was arrested in Egypt Nov. 2012, and is suspected of being released by the Muslim Brotherhood government of Mohamed Morsi in the fall of 2013.

The group Ansar al-Sharia, the al Qaeda-affiliated militia that US officials say took part in the Benghazi attack, operates several training camps set up to funnel jihadists to Syria's Islamist rebels. Obama's White House made no serious effort to eliminate them.

The Benghazi attack was carried out by dozens of Muslim jihadists on the 11th anniversary of the 9/11 attacks meant to devastate New York and Washington, D.C. and to "cripple" American resolve.

Benghazi US Embassy Islamic attack 9/11/2012:

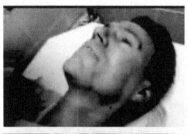

Chris Stevens
U.S. Ambassador to Libya

Khattala

Jamal

COVER OF THE NEW YORK POST
US drone witnessed attack on Benghazi

'THEY Military slow to respond
WATCHED
THEM DIE'

PAGES 4-7

Chapter Five

9/11 Speculations and Questions

..and then all of a sudden it started like -- It sounded like gunfire.
You know, bang, bang, bang, bang, bang.
*And then all of a sudden **three big explosions**.*
I went downstairs looking for my fellow workers,
*because at that time I didn't know the extent of the **explosion**.*
*I thought it was just an **explosion**,*
not that it was two planes that ran into the building.[1]

Arthur DelBianco

NBC *Today Show* interview, 9/12/2001
American Building Maintenance employee
Worked 15 years at the World Trade Center

The following speculations and statements from 9/11 theorists, experts, eyewitnesses, and/or official findings are not necessarily the views of the author or endorsers of this book.

9/11 Speculations and Questions:

Contrary to some conspiratorial allegations that Jews were pre-warned not to go to work that day, the number of Jews who died in the 9/11 attacks is estimated between 270 and 400.

In a newly released audio, two of New York City's bravest are heard to have made it up to where United Airlines Flight 175 impacted the 78th floor. Their voices where calm, they explain what was needed to help the many causalities and to put out the two small fires that they discovered.

The type of fire that these two NYC Firemen describe does not seem in sync with the commonly reported "inferno" that is blamed for melting the support beams that brought down the first ever steel high-rise skyscraper by extreme heat.

Louie Cacchioli, 51, another NYC firefighter, assigned to Engine 47 in Harlem, has stated on September 11, 2001: *"We were the first ones in the second tower after the plane struck. I was taking firefighters up in the elevator to the 24th floor to get in position to evacuate workers. On the last trip up a bomb went off. We think there were bombs set in the building. I had just asked another firefighter to stay with me, which was a good thing because we were trapped inside the elevator and he had the tools to get out."* [2]

Most Americans are unaware that a **3rd building collapsed** at 5:20pm on 9/11/2001, not more than 100 yards away from the North and South Towers, roughly 8 hours after they were leveled.

Building 7, known also as the "Solomon Brothers Building" had been evacuated, so there were no fatalities, which is why Building 7 garnishes little attention.

In its NIST Report (National Institute of Standards and Technology), the US Government maintains its explanation that "fire and natural causes" leveled this 47 story skyscraper made of steel in the World Trade Center Park. Yet, over 1,500 certified structural engineers maintain that it was a **controlled demolition** that felled this building.

FEMA aerial photos reveal WTC Building 6 and WTC Building 5 were closer to the Twin Towers (WTC Buildings 1&2) and more heavily damaged by falling debris, yet, their structures remain upright.

From videos of the collapse of Building 7,
the penthouse drops first prior to the collapse,
and it can be noted that windows, in a vertical line,

*near the location of first interior column line are blown out,
and reveal smoke from those explosions.
This occurs in a vertical line in symmetrical fashion an equal
distance in toward the center of the building from each end.
When compared to **controlled demolitions**,
one can see the similarities.* [3]

Robert F. Marceau
30 yr. structural engineer

*World Trade Center 7 appears to be a **controlled demolition**.
Buildings do not suddenly fall straight down by accident.* [4]

Steven L. Faseler
20 yr. structural engineer

*I agree the fire did not cause the collapse of the three buildings.
The most realistic cause of the collapse
is that the buildings were **imploded**.* [5]

Alfred Lee Lopez
48 yr. structural engineer

*WTC 7 Building **could not have collapsed** as a result
of internal **fire** and external debris. NO plane hit this building.
This is the only case of a steel frame building
collapsing through fire in the world.
The fire on this building was small and localized
therefore what is the cause?* [6]

Graham John Inman
London, England, structural engineer

*Near-freefall collapse **violates laws of physics**. Fire induced
collapse is not consistent with observed collapse mode..* [7]

David Scott

*It is very **suspicious** that fire brought down Building 7 yet the
Madrid hotel fire was still standing after 24 hours of fire. This is
very **suspicious** to me because I design buildings for a living.* [8]

Christopher Michael Bradbury

The symmetrical "collapse" due to asymmetrical damage is at odds with the principles of structural mechanics. [9]

Steven Francis Dusterwald

Photos of the steel, evidence about how the buildings collapsed, the unexplainable collapse of WTC 7, evidence of thermite in the debris as well as several other red flags, are quite troubling indications of well-planned and controlled demolition. [10]

Kamal S. Obeid
Structural engineer
UC Berkeley Masters degree in Engineering

In my opinion WTC 7 was with the utmost probability brought down by controlled demolition done by experts. [11]

Hugo Bachmann
Professor emeritus for structural analysis at ETH
Former Chairman of the Department of Structural Dynamics
Swiss Federal Institute of Technology

Plenty of clear photographs and videos show fires on floors 8, 11, 12, and 13, where the collapse began in Building 7. According to structural engineer experts, these office fires were not hot enough to melt a support column weighing 15,000 lbs. per floor to 1000° F.

Shortly after the core columns under the East Penthouse of Building 7 collapsed, the rest of the building collapsed mostly into its footprint in about 7 seconds.

Amazing online videos and resources of the 3rd building's collapse:

rememberbuilding7.org
www2.ae911truth.org/wtc7.php
wtc7.net
911research.wtc7.net/talks/towers
whatreallyhappened.com/WRHARTICLES/hijackers.html
911truth.org/former-explosives-loader-for-controlled-demolition/

Many eyewitnesses at Ground Zero on 9/11/2001 heard and felt **explosions** in the basement of the WTC Towers:

Anthony Saltalamacchia was a maintenance supervisor at the World Trade Center, overseeing over 100 American Building Maintenance employees:

On the morning of September 11th, I was in my office. I was just getting the work handed out to all the employees.
[Note: Mr. Saltalamacchia was in sub-basement B1 of North Tower 1, 1,100 feet below the airplane's impact point at floors 93-98.]
*We heard a **massive explosion** that was in the World Trade Center about 8:46 a.m. in the morning. The **explosion** came from -- I believe at first we believed that it came from the Mechanical Room.*
[NOTE: The Mechanical Room is below them in a lower sub-basement .]

*The amount of **explosions** I've heard from 8:46 until the time we got out was so many, at least **ten**. It was just like **multiple explosions** to where I felt like there were different grenades. That's what it sounded like, it was different grenades being set off in the building. It was like -- There was one major **explosion**, and then there was different **explosions** throughout that period of time until we got out.* [12]

WTC survivor, Phillip Morelli, construction worker at the World Trade Center for seven years, heard and felt explosions 4 stories below ground 15 minutes **before** the first plane hit the North Tower at 8:46am.

*As I'm walking by the main freight car of the building, in the corridor, that's when I got blown. I mean the impact of the **explosion**, from whatever happened, it threw me to the floor. And that's when everything started happening. It knocked me right to the floor. You didn't know what it was..*
[NOTE: Mr. Morelli was in the sub-basement of North Tower 1; 1,100 feet below the airplane's point of impact at floors 93-98.]

I was racing -- I was going towards the bathroom. All of a sudden. I opened the door. I didn't know it was a bathroom And all of a sudden a big impact happened again. And all the ceiling tiles were falling down. The light fixtures were falling, swinging out of the ceiling.

*And then all of a sudden it happened all over again. Building Two
got hit. I don't know that. I just know something else hit us to the
floor. Right in the basement you felt it. The walls were caving in.
Everything that was going on. I know of people that got killed in
the basement. People got reconstructive surgery
because the walls hit them in the face.* [13]

WTC survivor, Marlene Cruz, was a carpenter employed at the
World Trade Center for 15 years. ABC's Peter Jennings
interviewed Marlene Cruz on September 12, 2001:

*I work for the Trade Center. I'm one of the carpenters. And I was
gonna go do a job. And I got on the elevator, the freight elevator.
And I heard the first **explosion**. And the elevator blew up.
The doors blew up. And it dropped.
I was lucky that the elevator got caught between two floors.*

Peter Jennings: *Which floors?*

The B Levels..The basement levels.

[NOTE: Ms. Cruz was in the basement of the North Tower 1; 1,100 feet
below the airplane's point of impact at floors 93-98.]

*After the first **explosion** I was laying on the floor about 40
minutes. Well, I worked for the building for 15 years. I think I
know it from the back of my hand. Really I didn't expect this
bombing to occur after the first one* [1993 WTC bombing], *since I
was in the first one, also. But when I heard that **explosion** that's
the first thing I thought was; here we go again, another **bomb**.* [14]

WTC survivor, Mike Pecoraro, was a Stationary Engineer who
performed services in all of the buildings at the World Trade
Center. Mike and a co-worker were working in a sub-basement of
the North Tower when the first airplane hit. Mike was featured in a
2002 article of *Chief Engineer*:

*They had been told to stay where they were and "sit tight" until
the Assistant Chief got back to them. By this time, however, the
room they were working in began to fill with a white smoke.
We smelled kerosene..*

[NOTE: Mr. Pecoraro was in the sub-basement of the North Tower 1;
1,100 feet below the airplane's impact point at floors 93 to 98.]

The two men decided to ascend the stairs to Level C, to a small machine shop where Vito Deleo and David Williams were supposed to be working.

There was nothing there but rubble.
We're talking about a 50 ton hydraulic press? gone!..

The two men made their way to the parking garage, but found that it, too, was gone.

There were no walls, there was rubble on the floor,
and you can't see anything..

They decided to ascend two more levels to the building's lobby. As they ascended to the B Level, one floor above, they were astonished to see a steel and concrete fire door that weighed about 300 pounds, wrinkled up *"like a piece of aluminum foil"* and lying on the floor.

They got us again. [15]

(Referring to the terrorist attack at the center in 1993. Having been through that bombing, Mike recalled seeing similar things happen to the building's structure. He was convinced a bomb had gone off in the building.)

*I know there were **explosives** placed **below the trade center**. I helped a man to safety who is living proof, living proof the government story is a lie and a cover-up..I disagree 100% with the government story..I met with the 9/11 Commission behind closed doors and they essentially discounted everything I said regarding the use of **explosives** to bring down the North Tower..*
They just stared at me with blank faces
and didn't have any answers. [16]

William Rodriguez
9/11/2001 WTC Survivor
20-year American Building Maintenance employee who held the master key to the stairs

WTC Survivor, Felipe David, an Aramark Co. maintenance employee and office painter at the World Trade Center, recounts his story of being trapped in an elevator. Felipe was interviewed in 2002 by a Columbian TV station on the first 9/11 anniversary, recounting his experience while working in the basement of the North Tower on 9/11/2001:

*That day I was in the basement in sub-level 1 sometime after 8:30am. Everything happened so fast, everything moved so fast. The building started shaking after I heard the **explosion below**, dust was flying everywhere and all of a sudden it got real hot.*

Although severely burned on his face, arms and hands with skin hanging from his body like pieces of cloth, David picked himself up, running for help to the office where Willie Rodriguez and 14 others were huddled together.

*When I went in, I told them it was an **explosion**,*

said David, who was then helped out of the WTC by Rodriguez and eventually taken by ambulance to New York Hospital. [17]

WTC Survivor, Hursley Lever, an American Building Maintenance mechanic worked 12 years at the World Trade Center. NBC's *Today Show* interviewed Hursley Lever 9/12/2001:

*I was in the B-4 level. ... I heard a **bomb**.*
So, I says, 'Probably a transformer again blew up.'
So I step back, finish what I had to finish, and I started towards the door again. And there came a big blast with a big ball of fire. And that's when I got hit. It hit me right back down on the ground and I realized my ankle was shattered.

[NOTE: Mr. Lever was in sub-basement B4 of the North Tower 1; 1,100 feet below the airplane's impact point at floors 93-98.]

A Boston Globe article of Hursley Lever, 9/16/2001:

*Then I walk toward the door and heard a big **explosion**. And when I look, I see a ball of fire coming toward the door.*

Crawling and hopping from door to door, Lever prayed that the doors would not be locked. Lever said he never panicked, crediting his Army combat training for clear thinking in a crisis. When he emerged from the World Trade Center, Lever recalled, a police officer shouted to hit the ground. He made his way to a Secret Service-owned Bronco, where Lever was placed on his back. A two-way radio in the vehicle delivered even more unbelievable news: A second plane was about to strike the World Trade Center. On his back, Lever could only watch as the warning became reality. Several people left the Bronco and fled for their lives, Lever said, as flame, smoke, and debris rained around them. [18]

Dozens more credible eyewitness accounts confirm a verifiable consensus of what sounded and felt to them like a controlled demolition that felled the Twin Towers.

WTC victim, Edna Cintron, an Administrative Assistant at Marsh & McLennan in the North Tower, is videoed standing and waving for help from the gaping mouth where AA Flight 11 entered the North Tower. To some, this negates the theory that the buildings fell because of "inferno heat" at the point of impact that supposedly melted the support columns. Yet, here is a video that captures Edna Cintron standing and waving in that very spot: **http://thewebfairy.com/911/humanwaving/**.

Eyewitness video accounts of a 2nd and 3rd blast inside the buildings several minutes *after* both planes crashed that felled the Twin Tower buildings were filmed on the day of 9/11/2001:

www.youtube.com/watch?v=5IqSsTmWv7k&eurl=
www.youtube.com/watch?v=fnOeVQTSL9Y
www.youtube.com/watch?v=-qu07Gte-BU
www.youtube.com/watch?v=NLlMXkWW_LM

Hollywood A-list actor, James Woods, recalls an unnerving incident on an airplane shortly before 9/11/2001, involving the would-be future Islamic hijackers of the WTC air attack. In a recorded online interview, James Woods recounts telling the pilot of a pre-9/11 flight that he thought certain fellow passengers were planning to hijack his flight. Turns out, he was right. See James Woods interview online:

911truth.org/airport-security-ignored-pre-911-warnings-hijackers/

In a May 2003, a *Portuguese News* article reported that a marathon seminar of veteran US pilots, held in Washington, D.C., September 16-19, 2001, concluded that *"the flight crews of the four passenger airlines involved in the September 11th tragedy had no control over their aircraft."* This incredible story was never carried by the American press. [19]

Organizer of the high-profile symposium, Colonel Donn de Grand Pré (US Army Ret.), suggests an untold truth. (During the Ford and Carter administrations, de Grand Pré was considered to be the top US arms dealer in the Middle East.) His take on the four 9/11 airliners is unsettling,

"These planes were being piloted by remote control, probably an AWACS [Airborne Warning and Control System] *aircraft taking over that airplane, or airplanes; or drones, unmanned drone, and flying them at 5 and 8 G-force, that no pilot could withstand."* [20]
According to de Grand Pré, Boeing 757 and 767 are equipped with autonomous flight capability. They are the only two Boeing commuter aircraft capable of take off, flight to destination, and land, without a pilot at the controls.

These two are "intelligent" planes with software limits pre set, so that a pilot cannot cause passenger injury. For example, flight control systems prevent high G-force maneuvers via cockpit controls. Pilots are limited to 1.5 G-force maneuvers, so that a pilot does not end up breaking grandma's neck. The plane that hit the Pentagon was calculated by military personnel to have pulled between 5-7 G's in its final turn.

American Airlines pilot Kent Hill was a lifelong friend of Charles "Chic" Burlingame, the captain of AA Flight 77 that crashed into the Pentagon on 9/11/2001. They both graduated from the Naval Academy and flew F-4 Phantom missions in the Vietnam War. Hill insists in the same *Portuguese News* article that *"..all evidence points to the fact that the pilots and their crews had not taken any evasive action to resist the supposed hijackers. They had not attempted any sudden changes in flight path or nose-dive procedures – which led him to believe that they had no control over their aircraft."* [21]

Another swirl of government conspiracy asserts the aircraft(s) that crashed into the WTC were not commuter airlines, but a Air Force-owned windowless 757 fuel tanker.

Eyewitness Mark Burnback, a *FOX* news employee at Ground Zero, was quoted in *911 In Plane Site*, *"..Yeah, there was definitely a blue logo, like a circular logo on the front of the plane. It definitely **did not look like a commercial plane**. I didn't see any windows on the side..again, it was not any normal flight that I'd seen at an airport."* [22]

In the actual *911 Commission Report*, *"Within minutes, New York City's 911 system was flooded with eyewitness accounts of the event. Most callers correctly identified the target of the attack.* **SOME** *identified the plane as a commercial airliner."* Another witness included a female frantically yelling, *"That wasn't an American airplane that hit the building!"* [23]

A mysterious "Black Hole" left by a 125 feet wide plane that slammed into the side of the Pentagon on 9/11/2001 - was only **18 feet wide**. Flight 77 was 125 feet wide, 155 feet long, Boeing 757. What exactly *did* strike the Pentagon? A missile, perhaps?

Danielle O'Brien, one of the air traffic controllers at Dulles who reported seeing the aircraft at 9:25am, said, *"The speed, the maneuverability, the way that he turned, we all thought in the radar room, all of us experienced air traffic controllers, that that was a military plane."* [24]

Eyewitnesses who caught a glimpse of the actual crash from a 14th floor apartment in Pentagon City, and from a parked automobile, stated it, *"..made a shrill noise like a fighter plane..I was convinced it was a **missile**. It came in so fast it sounded nothing like an airplane..like a cruise **missile** with wings."* [25]

"Whatever" entered the Pentagon took out only the first two floors of the five-floor structure. Earliest photos of the crash prove this fact. Partial collapse of the upper floors occurred twenty minutes *after* initial impact. The official *911 Commission Report* includes a single photo of the "crash site" exhibiting the **latter photo version** of the collapsed building. The misleading(?) caption under the photo reads, *"The Pentagon, after being struck by American Airlines Flight 77."*

An interesting footnote to this controversy is an article in *Parade Magazine* reporting on Secretary of Defense Donald Rumsfeld in the Pentagon on October 12, 2001, who was explaining the various weapon options used by terrorists, referred to "the **missile** [used] to damage this building."[26] Freudian slip, perhaps?

Oddly enough, no photos of the Pentagon crash site show any sign of an airplane – no wings, no fuselage, no tail, no engine – nor any evidence that the front lawn was even scraped.

See a *CNN* reporter on the scene moments after the crash, who describes the site as anything but a plane crash:
youtube.com/watch?v=07Bn_CC_mrg

The most fascinating perspective on this is from Lt. General Dr. Paul K. Carlton, Jr (USAF, Ret.). A professing evangelical, Dr. Carlton is a fellow and former Air Force Governor of the American College of Surgeons, as well as former Surgeon General of the US Air Force. Playing a vital role in the Pentagon rescue effort on 9/11, Dr. Carlton led the first response team into the inner courtyard only five minutes after the attack.

Dr. Carlton paints a real-time picture for us. As the 757 Boeing hit the Pentagon with an estimated weight of 181,250 lbs, including 5,300 gallons of fuel, at a speed of 460 knots (100 knots above red line), only the fuselage and minimal section of the wings had time to enter the building as everything immediately disintegrated into tiny shards of metal averaging 1-2 inches in size. Much of this debris is visible in photos which appear in the *Pentagon Building Performance Report,* published by the American Society of Civil Engineers.

Retired Army Lt. Colonel, Frank Probst, a West Point graduate and decorated Vietnam War veteran, recalls being near the Pentagon heliport when the crash occurred and seeing fine pieces of wing debris floated down around him.

Simply put, the plane wings did not fully enter the building. The largest structural piece of the plane, the landing gear, would be expected to travel the furthest, and it did. The detached landing gear of AA Flight 77 punched a hole through the E, D, and C rings of the Pentagon before bouncing off the B ring outer wall and coming to rest in an alley.

The rarely discussed "crash" of UA Flight 93 in Shanksville, PA, offers a dispiriting theory of its destruction by an F-16 fighter jet. Yet, one passenger's words of insurmountable courage in the face of likely death would inspire an entire nation.

A remarkable conversation on 9/11 between Todd Beamer and Lisa Jefferson, a telephone switchboard operator riveted all of us. The immortalized words are: *"Let's Roll."*

See Jefferson's *CBS* interview online: **youtube.com/watch?v=H-viMzr2nac**

Jefferson was in a suburb of Chicago, at the headquarters of the GTE phone company, when she took the call that, she now says, changed her life. Beamer didn't want to worry his pregnant wife, so he calmly called GTC, the company that provides the telephone service on United Airlines flights. Beamer and Jefferson talked for 13 minutes, during which they recited together the Lord's Prayer and Psalm 23.

The aircraft had been re-routed by terrorists when Beamer called GTC and was now on its way to Washington, D.C. Beamer, along with other courageous passengers, planned to re-take control of the plane from the hijackers.

It was at 9:30am when three men with red bandanas suddenly rushed towards the cockpit and air traffic controllers in Cleveland picked up this message: *"Hey, get out of here!"* The end had begun.

Cleveland then picked up an announcement, probably from terrorist Ziad Jarrah having flipped the wrong switch, with a message he thought he was delivering over the PA: *"There is a bomb on board, we are meeting their demands, we are heading back to the airport."* This, as Jarrah knew, was nonsense. Instead, the plane began to climb. [27]

A cockpit tape recording on a 30-minute loop, begins with wailing and screaming, someone pleading not to be hurt or killed. Somebody else chokes. According to one passenger, both pilots were seen lying motionless on the floor just outside the first-class curtain. Their throats were cut. Within six minutes, UA Flight 93 had changed course and was heading for Washington, D.C.

Final words of love and goodbyes were released through digital airwaves, 23 from airphones, others by personal mobiles, with passengers passing their cell phones to strangers. Through these calls, those aboard UA Flight 93 learned the full scope of what was happening that morning.

At that point, Todd Beamer's voice went up a little bit as he said to Jefferson, *"We're going down, we're turning round.. Oh, I don't know, Jesus, please help us."* The two chatted about Beamer's family; his sons Drew and David. Then he said, *"My wife is expecting,"* so we talked. They discovered Jefferson and his wife shared the same Christian name. The conversation went from the sublime to the practical, says Jefferson, *"He wanted me to recite the Lord's Prayer with him."* Then came the Psalm, with - according to Jefferson - a number of other passengers now joining in, as though for a last rite. [28]

From that point, Jefferson tells Beamer he was going to have to go out on faith because they were talking about jumping the guy with the bomb. Beamer was still holding the phone but not talking to Jefferson. Turning his head away, he could be heard saying to someone else, *"You ready. Okay, let's roll."* [29]

"We're all running to first class", flight attendant Sandy Bradshaw could be heard saying, implying the rebellion had begun in Mark Bingham's compartment, seated near the front of the plane. Between rows 30 and 34, the revolt had brewed along with a pot of boiling water, which Bradshaw was planning to splash into a hijacker's face.

The standard manual advising pilots to be careful and appease hijackers was about to be ripped up, along with the history of hijacking protocol. The terrorists had a serious fight coming. The hijackers chose their flight plan poorly. Glick was a 6'1" judo champion; Bingham a rugby player; Burnett had been a college quarterback. Among the other passengers, Louis Nacke was a weightlifter. William Cashman was a former paratrooper.

An analyst indication of the recording pinpointed the scuffle began not at the back of the plane but at the front - where Bingham was sitting. There was talk of "rushing the hijackers." Glick, in a third call, asked "Lyz" if she thought it was a good idea. She said she did.

From 9:57am, the cockpit recorder picks up sounds of extreme fighting in an aircraft losing control at 30,000 feet - the crash of trolleys, dishes being hurled and smashed. The terrorists scream at each other to hold the door against what is obviously a siege of the cabin. A passenger cries, *"Let's get them!"* There is more screaming, then an apparent breach of the cabin.. *"Give it to me!"* shouts a passenger, apparently about to seize the controls. [30]

Stretched across the rolling green pastures of Somerset County, PA, gawking farmers and commuters watched a huge commercial plane rock and sway, and then meet the ground in an earth-shattering cloud of black mushroom smoke.

See an online video seconds after Flight 93 crashed: **youtube.com/watch?t=1&v=Pvo4ixnnILQ**

A January 27, 2002, a story in the *Washington Post* alleged Vice President Cheney gave three separate go-aheads for US fighter jet engagement on UA Flight 93. See Cheney's video admission online: **youtube.com/watch?v=7vV3fjfeb9Q**

A relevant press story in the *Pittsburgh Post Gazette*, September 13, 2001, confirmed plane debris and human remains were discovered well over 6 miles leading to the crash crater in Shanksville, PA. The *Boston Herald* quoted Deputy Secretary of Defense, Paul Wolfowitz, stating, *"And in fact we were already tracking in on that plane that crashed in Pennsylvania. I think it was the heroism of the passengers on board that brought it down, but the Air Force was in a position to do so if we had had to."* [31]

CNN's account of Donald Rumsfeld's Christmas Eve address to the troops in Baghdad on December 28, 2004, states, *"..the people who attacked the United States in New York, shot down the plane over Pennsylvania."* [32]

High ranking military personnel have gone on record, under secret identity, to affirm that after the passenger's unsuccessful takeover of UA Flight 93, the plane was actually shot down by military jets. The plan was to go with the story of the passenger's takeover attempt with the media.

Ernie Stuhl, the mayor of Shanksville: *"I know of two people -- I will not mention names -- that heard a missile. They both live very close, within a couple of hundred yards... This one fellow's served in Vietnam and he says he's heard them, and he heard one that day."* He adds that based on what he has learned; F-16s were "very, very close." [33]

Laura Temyer of Hooversville: *"I didn't see the plane but I heard the plane's engine. Then I heard a loud thump that echoed off the hills and then I heard the plane's engine. I heard two more booms and didn't hear the plane's engine anymore after that..I think it was shot down"* (she insists that people she knows in state law enforcement have privately told her the plane was shot down, and that decompression sucked objects from the aircraft, explaining why there was a wide debris field). [34]

An unnamed witness interviewed on *Cleveland News Channel 5*, 9/11/2001, says he hears two loud bangs before watching the plane take a downward turn of nearly 90 degrees. [35]

Eyewitness Linda Shepley hears a **loud bang** and sees the plane bank to the side. She sees the plane wobbling right and left, at a low altitude of roughly 2,500 feet, when suddenly the right wing dips straight down, and the plane plunges into the earth. Linda says she had an unobstructed view of Flight 93's final two minutes. [36]

Well-founded uncertainty looms in a cloudy cabal over official government reports. *The Record* newspaper (Bergen County, NJ) reported that five eyewitnesses reported seeing a second plane at the Flight 93 crash site. Although government officials insist there was never any pursuit of Flight 93, they were informed the flight was suspected of having been hijacked at 9:16am, fully 50 minutes before the plane came down. [37]

Eyewitness, John Fleegle, shares his unofficial testimony in an online video of a "plane being shot out of the sky" in Shanksville, PA, on 9/11/2001: **youtube.com/watch?v=LWcdSyyppHI.**

Less than a minute before the Flight 93 crash rocked the countryside, Susan Mcelwain sees a small white jet with rear engines and no discernible markings swoop low over her minivan near an intersection and disappear over a hilltop, nearly clipping the tops of trees lining the ridge. She later adds, *"There's no way I imagined this plane - it was so low it was virtually on top of me. It was white with no markings but it was **definitely military**, it just had that look. It had two rear engines, a big fin on the back like a spoiler on the back of a car and with two upright fins at the side. I haven't found one like it on the internet. It definitely wasn't one of those executive jets. The FBI came and talked to me and said there was no plane around... But I saw it and it was there before the crash and it was 40 feet above my head. They did not want my story - nobody here did."* [38]

Dennis Decker and Rick Chaney witnessed, *"As soon as we looked up* [after hearing the Flight 93 crash], *we saw a midsized jet flying low and fast. It appeared to make a loop or part of a circle, and then it turned fast and headed out."* Decker and Chaney described the plane as a Learjet type, with engines mounted near the tail and painted white with no identifying markings. *"It was a jet plane, and it had to be flying real close when that 757 went down. If I was the FBI, I'd find out who was driving that plane."* [39]

Jim Brandt sees a small plane with no markings stay about one or two minutes over the crash site before leaving. Tom Spinelli recalls, *"I saw the white plane. It was flying around all over the place like it was looking for something. I saw it before and after the crash."* The FBI later says this was a Fairchild Falcon 20 business jet, directed after the crash to fly from 37,000 feet to 5,000 feet and obtain the coordinates for the crash site to help rescuers. Yet officials have never identified the pilot nor explained why he was still airborne roughly 30 minutes after the government ordered all aircraft to land at the closest airport. [40]

A British newspaper later strongly suggests that a fighter jet passed near Flight 93 well before it crashed. *"Further verification that some kind of military aircraft was operating in the area is scientifically irrefutable. A sonic boom - caused by supersonic flight - was picked up by an earthquake monitoring station in southern Pennsylvania, 60 miles from Shanksville."* [41]

At 9:58am on 9/11/2001, a Flight 93 male passenger calls 911 from a bathroom on the plane, crying, *"We're being hijacked, we're being hijacked!"* The dispatcher reported that *"he* [the passenger] *heard some sort of explosion and saw white smoke coming from the plane and we lost contact with him."* Investigators believe this was Edward Felt, the only passenger not accounted for on phone calls. He was sitting in first class, so he probably was in the bathroom near the front of the plane. At one point he appears to have peeked out the bathroom door. The mentions of smoke and explosions of the recording of his call are now denied by official government reports. The person who took Felt's call is not allowed to speak to the media. [42]

CBS television reported at approximately 10:06am at some point before the crash that two F-16 fighters were tailing Flight 93. Shortly after 9/11, a flight controller in New Hampshire ignores a ban on controllers speaking to the media, and it is reported he claims *"that an F-16 fighter closely pursued Flight 93... the F-16 made 360-degree turns to remain close to the commercial jet,"* the employee said. *"He must've seen the whole thing"*, the employee said of the F-16 pilot's view of Flight 93's crash. [43]

At 2pm on 9/11/2001, F-15 fighter pilot Maj. Daniel Nash returns to base around this time, after chasing Flight 175 and patrolling the skies over New York City. He says that when he got out of the plane, *"he was told that a military F-16 had shot down a fourth airliner in Pennsylvania, a report that turned out to be incorrect."* [44]

Kathy Blades was in her small summer cottage about a quarter-mile from the impact site. Blades and her son ran outside after the crash and saw the jet, with sleek back wings and an angled cockpit, race overhead. *"My son said, 'I think we're under attack!'"* She said she was so shocked by the crash she can't say exactly how long after the impact it was. [45]

As FBI and conventional wisdom have said the plane was mostly obliterated by the roughly 500 mph impact, an engine - or at least a 1,000-pound piece of one - was found a considerable distance *away* from the crater. Ernie Stuhl, 77 year old WWII veteran in 2001 and Mayor of Shanksville, said it was found in the woods just west of the crash. This information is intriguing to shoot-down theory proponents, since heat-seeking, air-to-air Sidewinder missiles aboard an F-16 would likely target one of the Boeing 757's two large engines.

There was also widely scattered debris in the vicinity and further afield. Considerable debris washed up more than two miles away at Indian Lake, and a canceled check and brokerage statement from the plane was found in a deep valley some eight miles away that week. [46]

"I think it was shot down," said Dennis Mock, who was not an eyewitness but lives closest to the crash site on the west side. *"That's what people around here think."* [47]

One thing is for absolute certain: Shanksville, PA, was forever etched into America's psychic map on the morning of September 11, 2001, when United Airlines Flight 93 slammed nose-down into the edge of a barren strip-mine moonscape a couple of miles outside of town.

The 5 brave passengers who spear-headed the plane's coup (Glick, Beamer, Bingham, Burnett, Nacke – all Caucasian males) could not have done a better job in picking Shanksville, PA, to bring down the plane. The nearest sizable town, Somerset, is 10 miles away on winding back-country roads, where a visitor might encounter as many dead raccoons as vehicles. Nestled along a creek bed in the rolling Allegheny foothills, Shanksville is a small cluster of red-brick homes and flag-draped front porches. The only commercial enterprise, a convenience store called Ida's, also rents videos and has the only ATM for miles around.

Yet, what happened there is the stuff of legends. Todd Beamer's *"Let's Roll!"* was shortly thereafter adopted by President Bush, became a sports team rally cry, and was spliced into bumper music rotations on the Rush Limbaugh radio show.

As a confused and grief-stricken nation was grasping to comprehend multiple 9/11 attacks on the same day, UA Flight 93 passengers provided for all Americans a measure of victory in the midst of unfathomable defeat – sacrificing their own lives so that others might live. This is the real America.

Comprehensive websites questioning what really happened on 9/11/2001:

mycountryrightorwrong.net/23informativewebsiteson911.htm
patriotsquestion911.com/professors.html#MacQueen
http://911review.com/attack/wtc/impacts.html
http://911research.wtc7.net/wtc/attack/wtc2.html

An online video showing the crater of the UA Flight 93 "crash site" has been in existence since **1994**:

youtube.com/watch?v=Lluph4ouX-c

Recommended Reading:
Among the Heroes by Jere Longman
Let's Roll! By Lisa Beamer (Todd Beamer's wife)

This one tops the *"huh?"* list..
In 2010, plans for building an Islamic mosque and "cultural center" at Ground Zero drew outrage in NY City. The controversy was brought into national view primarily through breaking news coverage from conservative talk radio hosts: Limbaugh, Hannity, Ingraham, as well as online most-clicked news outlets: *Drudge Report, wnd.com, christianpost.com,* etc. Mainstream media *NBC, CBS, ABC, CNN, MSNBC*, et al, sheepishly caught up to the story due to a tsunami of public patriotic outcry.

Americans who respect the memory of 9/11 victims saw the plan to install a Muslim mosque at Ground Zero as a clear provocation.

The $100M twelve story resort-mosque with a swimming pool would be located on hallowed ground just two blocks away from where the Twin Towers stood.

Retired New York Fire Department Deputy Chief Jim Riches, whose 29-year-old son Jim, a firefighter, was killed on 9/11, called it *"a slap in the face of the* [victim's] *families"*. Ted Sjurseth, a founder of *America's 9/11 Foundation*, a Virginia-based support group for first responders, called the mosque plan *"a stick in the eye."* [48]

The Islamic center project was the brainchild of Feisel Abdul Rauf, a New York imam, and Daisy Khan, executive director of the *American Society for Muslim Advancement*. Known as Cordoba House, the Islamic center's mosque would accommodate up to 1,500 worshippers of Allah on Fridays. The complex would also include a "performance space" and a basketball court. Of course, it would be open to non-Muslims as well, encouraging curiosity seekers.

The "performance space" would be used to perform *what* exactly, I wonder. How to jihad? How to execute infidels? How to infiltrate the US political system with Sharia Law? Hmmm.

Fewer political firestorms have consumed more oxygen. Liberals embracing cultural "diversity" and "understanding" from their PC-scarred psyche are viewed by conservatives as progressives who just don't "get it". The "Park51 Project" ultimately was rightly cast as an insult to 9/11 victims and their families.

Former-Democrat-now-moderate-Republican New York Mayor, Michael Bloomberg, who conveniently switched parties in 2001 to become mayor following Republican Rudy Giuliani's final term, was one of the lone voices in favor of the project. Advocates of the mosque asserted their best clairvoyant assurances that the Park51 Muslim cultural center planners had no ulterior motives.

The Park51 Project sought IRS approval to be designated as a tax-exempt 501(c)3 nonprofit organization. Without the nonprofit designation, Park51 would be hard-pressed to raise anywhere near the $100 million needed for the project.

From the start, developer Sharif El-Gamal did not seek any input from 9/11 victim's families. He called opposition to the project part of a *"campaign against Muslims."* [49]

With help from Mayor Bloomberg, opening of a much scaled-down version of Park51 (a temporary 4,000-square-foot center located two blocks from the WTC) was celebrated by a small orchestra of Middle Eastern instruments in September 2011. Emphasizing "interfaith dialogue," one floor is dedicated as a Muslim prayer space.

As of August 2014, the owner proposes to complete the project in a three story museum instead of the original 13 story cultural center.

As if we need more 9/11 controversy..

As America marked the 10th anniversary of the 2001 terrorist attacks on the World Trade Center, the World Trade Center property owners filed a lawsuit in 2011 in New York Federal court against Massport, American Airlines, United Airlines and other others for lax security measures on the day of 9/11/2001.

Judge Alvin K. Hellerstein has permitted WTC property owners to seek $2.8 billion in damages, half of which was recovered under insurance. In 2013, Judge Hellerstein put a stop to more demands after WTC owners received already $5 billion in damage relief.

A spokesman for Silverstein Properties said the developer was "deeply disappointed" by the ruling and would appeal. Silverstein remains committed to ongoing construction projects on the site.

Attorney Roger Podesta, defending companies United Airlines Inc., US Airways Inc., American Airlines Inc. and its parent company, AMR Corp., argued that making aviation companies pay would amount to double compensation.

Podesta projected an $8.5 billion total recovery request would be more than two and a half times the fair value of the buildings that fell. The trade center owners are claiming it has cost more than $7 billion to replace the twin towers and more than $1 billion to replace the third trade center building that fell (Building 7).

A flight recorder (black box), invented in 1953 by David Warren and made of fireproof titanium steel, is not actually black in color. These days they are commonly bright orange. Required on all passenger planes, there are always two: a flight data recorder that keeps track of a plane's speed, altitude, and course maneuvers; and a cockpit voice recorder which keeps a continuous recording of the last 30 minutes of conversation inside a plane's cockpit.

These devices are constructed to be extremely durable, and are installed in a plane's tail section, where they are least likely to suffer damage on impact. They are designed to withstand up to 30 minutes of heat up to 1800° (more than they would have faced in the twin towers crashes), and to survive a crash at full speed into the ground. UA Flight 93 crashed in PA going 500 mph.

If a plane crashes into the water, the ULB (underwater locator beacon), which doubles as a carrying handle, sends out an ultrasonic pulse that cannot be heard by human ears but is readily detectable by sonar and acoustical locating equipment. There is a submergence sensor on the side of the beacon that looks like a bull's-eye. When water touches this sensor, the beacon is activated.

A mystery is why the black boxes were made available for the 2 planes that crashed into the Pentagon and Shanksville, PA; but not for the 2 planes that crashed into the Twin Towers, even though 3 of the 4 black boxes were found by 2 NY City firefighters, Mike Bellone and Nicholas De Masi.

The cleanup of the World Trade Center was meticulous, with even tiny bone fragments and bits of human tissue being discovered in WTC debris. In 2013, *CBS* news reported only 1,634 people have been identified (59%) out of roughly 2,750 people who died in at the World Trade Center on 9/11/2001.[50]

The FBI and *9-11 Commission Report* states none of the recording devices from the two planes that hit the Twin Towers were ever recovered. Yet, an unnamed source at the **National Transportation Safety Agency** which has the job of analyzing the boxes' data, said, *"Off the record, we had the boxes. You'd have to get the official word from the FBI as to where they are, but we worked on them here."* [51]

Why the main intel and law enforcement agencies of the US Government do not want the public to know its content only further fuels conspiracy theories that abound. The easiest way to squash rumors of the planes being pilotless military aircrafts, or that the planes had little to do with the Twin Towers collapse, would be more openness by the US Government.

Building 7:

Flight Recorder (black box):

UA Flight 93:

US Pentagon:

Park 51 Project: (Sharif El-Gamal, Michael Bloomberg)

Chapter Six

America's War on Terror

This mass terrorism is the new evil in our world today.
It is perpetrated by fanatics who are utterly indifferent
to the sanctity of human life,
and we the democracies of this world are going to have to
come together and fight it together. [1]

Tony Blair
British Prime Minister, 1997-2007

Islam is a religion in which God requires you to send your son
to die for him.
Christianity is a faith in which God sends his son
to die for you. [26]

John Ashcroft
US Attorney General, 2001-2005

The morning of December 2, 2015, San Bernardino, CA, marked the 75th Islamic-inspired terrorist attack on American soil since 9/11/2001. It was the 12th terrorist plot in 2015 - the largest number of attacks on the US in a single year since 2001, according to data compiled by Heritage Foundation's Riley Walters December 8, 2015 issue brief #4496 on terrorism.

Breaking news in September 2015 exposed the former witless Clinton White House for suppression of evidence (Clinton's cable to Iran) that proved Iran's direct responsibility for the deadly 1996 Khobar Towers terrorist bombing which killed 19 American servicemen.

Impeached President Bill Clinton's foreign policy of appeasement to "grease" relations with the Iranian government was upset by reality via FBI Director Louis Freeh, when he first presented evidence of Iran's direct responsibility in terrorist acts that killed Americans. This information was substantiated by real-time confessions of a half-dozen Saudi co-conspirators, who revealed they got their passports from the Iranian embassy in Damascus, reported to a top Iranian general, and were trained by Iran's Revolutionary Guard (IRGC).

Among the most incriminating evidence is a top-secret cable sent in the summer of 1999 from Clinton to Iran's new and more moderate president at the time, Mohammad Khatami, acknowledging that the US believed Iran had participated in the Khobar Towers truck bombing, killing 498 (19 Americans).

For fear it would lead to an outcry of reprisal, "sleep-meister" Clinton stuffed all evidence from public view. Doing his job to protect Americans, Freeh sought the Clinton White House's help to gain access to the Saudi suspects. He was repeatedly thwarted by Clinton's passive-aggressive stiff arm. When Freeh succeeded by going around Clinton and returned with hard core evidence, it was dismissed as "hearsay," and Freeh was asked not to spread it around, so as to not "rock the boat" with Iran.

"The bottom line was they weren't interested. They were not at all responsive to it," Mr. Freeh described the Clinton administration's stifling of evidence linking Iran to Khobar. [2]

When Freeh exposed similar Clinton-led failures in his book about his tenure with the FBI, Clinton supporters decades earlier slammed Freeh, claiming evidence against Iran was inconclusive, and that the White House never tried to thwart the probe.

Now that the recently untold truth has vindicated Freeh, it became obvious Bill Clinton deserved impeachment for more than just lying about an intern's blue dress stained with his loin juice. His derelict presidency also betrayed the #1 Constitutional duty of his oath to protect all Americans.

Thankfully, a real adult was elected next President to the United States Oval Office in 2000.

America needed a strong leader to combat the Koran-inspired bullies who beat down our fellow brothers and sisters, and injured the American spirit, on September 11, 2001.

During a State of the Union address to Congress, September 20, in 2001, President George W. Bush marked the start of America's War on Terror, a phrase the President coined in his speech. *"Our war on terror begins with Al Qaida, but it does not end there,"* he said. *"It will not end until every terrorist group of global reach has been found, stopped, and defeated."* [3]

On May 23, 2013, President Barak Hussein Obama publicly announced America's global War on Terror is "over" - only that it's not. Delay of troop withdrawals backtracked Obama's delusive campaign promise(s) to voters in 2008 and 2012 that he will bring home all US troops. As of Oct. 2015, Obama proclaimed 9,800 troops left in Afghanistan through 2016 would train Afghan troops and "go after" al Qaeda. It clearly shows Obama's foreign policy nescience while pandering to harvest votes during election years.

As America's War on Terror began in 2001, many US citizens felt united to follow President George W. Bush's lead to cut off US Government funding to terrorist-sponsoring nations. US Congress passed laws immediately after 9/11/2001, refusing to grant US loans or federal aid funds to Middle Eastern nations, such as Iraq, who are factually known to grant safe-harbor to Islamic terrorist leaders, militants, factions, and training camps.

Several gas companies, such as Exxon, Shell, Speedway, Amoco, Chevron, Texaco, and Citgo, purchase their gas and oil from OPEC (Organization of the Petroleum Exporting Countries), namely, Middle Eastern oil companies owned or controlled by sworn enemies of the United States of America.

As leaders of these countries vomit their public glee and blame onto America for being attacked on 9/11, they stand to profit financially as their gasoline product is inconceivably made readily available within our own country's gas pumps.

So, many Americans decided to boycott OPEC oil at the pump.

Instead, conscientious Americans purchased their gasoline from BP, which stands for British Petroleum, and Hess, who do not directly purchase natural gas from OPEC. Sunoco, Sinclair, Flying J, Murphy Oil USA, Maverick, and Valero also do not primarily purchase natural gas from OPEC, nor Middle Eastern oil. Great Britain, our ally in the War on Terror, owns BP gas stations.

To say that President George W. Bush "lied" about WMDs (weapons of mass destruction) in Iraq to get the US into a "war over oil" in the Middle East is lazy, ill-informed, template-driven, false reporting.

The National Intelligence Estimate delivered to President Bush and Congress said there was a 90% certainty of WMDs in Iraq. Democrat George Tenet, the Clinton CIA director who continued to serve under Bush, said the case for WMDs was a "slam dunk."

Leading Democrat Senators John Kerry, Hillary Clinton, Chuck Schumer, Harry Reid and Joe Biden all looked at the intelligence reports and voted to authorize military force. Sen. Jay Rockefeller (D-WV) argued strongly for the war. Then, years later, when it wasn't going so well, he published a highly politicized report ripping Bush. Here is the truth untold..

The No. 2 official in Saddam Hussein's air force, General Georges Sada, acknowledges Iraq moved chemical weapons of mass destruction into Syria before the Iraq War began by loading the weapons into civilian aircraft in which the passenger seats were removed.[28] Read Sada's book, *Saddam's Secrets*.

*One way or another, we are determined to deny Iraq the capacity to develop **weapons of mass destruction** and the missiles to deliver them. That is our bottom line.* [4]
President Bill Clinton, February 4, 1998

*If Saddam rejects peace and we have to use force, our purpose is clear. We want to seriously diminish the threat posed by **Iraq's weapons of mass destruction** program.* [5]
President Bill Clinton, February 17, 1998

*He will use those **weapons of mass destruction** again, as he has ten times since 1983.* [6]
Sandy Berger, February 18, 1998
Clinton National Security Advisor

*We urge you, after consulting with Congress, and consistent with US Constitution and laws, to take necessary action (including, if appropriate, air and missile strikes on suspect Iraqi sites) to respond effectively to the threat posed by Iraq's refusal to end its **weapons of mass destruction** programs.* [7]

Tom Dashle(D-SD), John Kerry(D-MA), Dianne Feinstein(D-CA)
Joint-Letter to President Clinton, October 9, 1998

*Saddam Hussein has been engaged in the development of **weapons of mass destruction** technology...and he has made a mockery of the weapons inspection process.* [8]

Nancy Pelosi (D-CA), December 16, 1998

*Hussein has.. chosen to spend his money on building **weapons of mass destruction** and palaces for his cronies.* [9]

Madeline Albright, November 10, 1999
Clinton Administration Secretary of State

*We know that he has stored secret supplies of **biological and chemical weapons** throughout his country.*
*Iraq's search for **weapons of mass destruction** has proven impossible to deter and we should assume that it will continue for as long as Saddam is in power.* [10]

Al Gore (D-TN), September 23, 2002

*We have known for many years that Saddam Hussein is seeking and developing **weapons of mass destruction**.* [11]

Ted Kennedy (D-MA), September 27, 2002

*I will be voting to give the President the authority to use force – if necessary – to disarm Saddam Hussein because I believe that a deadly arsenal of **weapons of mass destruction** in his hands is a real and grave threat to our security.* [12]

John Kerry (D-MA), October 9, 2002

President Bush's famed "16 words" in his 2003 State of the Union address is used as a whip by Democrats to daily flail Bush's Presidential legacy, purporting that "Bush lied" to the American people: *"The British government has learned that Saddam Hussein recently sought significant quantities of uranium from Africa."* [13]

Latching onto a disgruntled US Diplomat's claim to the contrary, leftist mainstream news talking-heads cheered the Diplomat's words as divine truth.

The former US *dip*-lomat, Joe Wilson, best known for his 2002 trip to Niger to investigate allegations that Saddam Hussein was attempting to purchase yellowcake uranium (the seed material used for higher-grade nuclear enrichment and weapons) is known for his New York Times op-ed hit-piece, *"What I Didn't Find in Africa,"* and the alleged leaking of information pertaining to his wife Valerie Plame's identity as a CIA agent.

A popular 2003 *Time* magazine hit-piece "Bush and Iraq: Follow the Yellow Cake War" concluded - - no yellowcake equals no WMDs equals bogus basis for the war in Iraq. *Time* hoisted Joe Wilson on its shoulders as a "man who told the truth to power", referring often to Bush's yellowcake "lie."

Wired magazine's contributing editor Noah Shachtman -- a nonresident fellow at the liberal Brookings Institution -- researched 400,000 *WikiLeak* documents released in October 2010. Here's what he found: *"WikiLeaks' newly-released Iraq war documents reveal that for years afterward, U.S. troops continued to find chemical weapons labs, encounter insurgent specialists in toxins and uncover weapons of mass destruction ... Chemical weapons, especially, did not vanish from the Iraqi battlefield. Remnants of Saddam's toxic arsenal, largely destroyed after the Gulf War, remained. Jihadists, insurgents and foreign (possibly Iranian) agitators turned to these stockpiles during the Iraq conflict -- and may have brewed up their own deadly agents. In 2008, our military shipped out of Iraq -- on 37 flights in 3,500 barrels -- what even The Associated Press called 'the last major remnant of Saddam Hussein's nuclear program:' 550 metric tons of the supposedly nonexistent yellowcake."* [14]

Square that with what inflammatory Democratic National Chairman Howard Dean said in April 2004: *"There were no weapons of mass destruction."* MSNBC's petulant Rachel Maddow goes even further, insisting, against the overwhelming evidence to the contrary, that *"Saddam Hussein was not pursuing weapons of mass destruction."* [15]

The *WikiLeaks* de facto declassification of privileged material makes this case closed: Saddam Hussein possessed weapons of mass destruction -- and intended to restart his program once the heat of war was off. Yet, President Bush is still hammered today by millennials' peacenik mantra, *"Bush lied. People died."*

The liberal's conspiracy theorists have been proven false since Britain's **Butler Commission** reviewed its government pre-war intelligence on Iraq and concluded "the British government had intelligence from several different sources indicating that this visit was for the purpose of acquiring uranium."

It was again proven false when our own **US Senate Intelligence Committee** also concluded, in July 2004, that Saddam Hussein had indeed sought uranium from Niger.

Yet another lie on top of this is the absurd implication that the news media were *too soft* on President Bush during the war.

During the Iraq War buildup, even as overwhelming majorities in both houses of Congress authorized the use of force, 59 percent of the sound bites aired by the evening newscasts were anti-war, 29 percent pro-war.

To take one of innumerable examples, in 2006 President Bush had about the same approval ratings that Obama suffered in 2014. The network news both commissioned far more polls when Bush stood to suffer, and reported on the Bush results far more.

Again, this isn't even close: The score was 52 to 2, as in 52 mentions of low Bush approval ratings versus 2 mentions of (even lower, at times) Obama approval ratings.

In every Gallup poll this century, more Americans called the media "too liberal" than "too conservative." The numbers were 45 to 15 in 2003, the year of the Iraq invasion. In 2008, as Obama was being elected, it was 47 to 13. In fall 2015, it was 44 to 19.

Thanks to Hollywood polemicists (ie: David Letterman) and media clowns (John Stewart and Stephen Colbert), the myth that "Bush lied" has caught on, and now a majority of Americans believe it.

Yet, if you point out that Bill O'Reilly's audience is just as well informed as *NPR*'s (as a Pew poll found), or that Sarah Palin never said, *"I can see Russia from my house"* (that was Saturday Night Live's Tina Fey), you're just a buzz-kill, or a "truth-er."

The difference is that *NBC* news anchor Brian "Pinocchio" Williams has become a joke for fabricating lies on air while looking straight into the eye of America on camera. Jon Stewart is a liar for the way he told his jokes.

Truth is, during the 2004 reelection of President Bush, military vets polled by Bush-belligerent *CBS*, preferred Bush (54%) over John Kerry (41%) as Commander in Chief.

In the same poll, of the *civilian* voters polled, 51% approved of Bush's handling of the War on Terror.[16] Unlike the daily onslaught of negative-focused, template-driven, critical news stories by all major media and entertainment outlets, Bush's real-time wartime approval rating among low-information voters was still favorable.

President Bush was internally known as a personable, caring soul; visiting veteran hospitals, amputee victims and bereaving families; often shedding tears privately with families of victims, as well as publicly in speeches.

Bush carefully braved the tough decisions of war time reality, felt empathetically, and faced squarely those who suffered the consequences of war with warm comfort and understanding as well as any war-time President could.

In 2014, former President George W. Bush visited Texas Health Presbyterian Hospital in Dallas, the first hospital to diagnose an Ebola patient.

Unlike Barack Obama, President Bush participates in golf fundraisers, bike rides (Warrior 100K, **bushcenter.org/military-service-initiative/w100k**), and personal visits, all for vets and amputees, spreading cheer. Bush never has been a President of limitless faults as leftist media will always portray him, but a President of grounded humanity, imperfect, yet always mature.

There were 4,417 American military deaths during the impeached presidency of Bill Clinton from 1993-1996. After the toughest first half of the President Bush-led War on Terror from 2004-2007, there were 3,100 American soldiers killed fighting in Iraq. [17]

Thanks to spite-filled, media-consensus reporting doggedly bent on putting the Bush administration under a cloud of suspicion, it was sadly forgotten that our enemy killed about the same number of Americans *in one day* on our own soil.

To be fair, there were a total of 7,500 military deaths during the entire impeached Clinton presidency. During the first 6 years of the Bush administration, the number was 8,792.[18] The difference is, Bush was fighting a full-scale war. Clinton was not. Name for me any war-time US President that wouldn't love to embrace Bush's low war-time fatality statistics compared to previous United States wars.

US War American Fatalities:

American Revolutionary War = **25,000**
War of 1812 = **15,000**
Mexican-American War = **13,283**
Civil War = **664,035**   *Union 364,511 / Confederate 299,524
WWI = **116,516**
WWII = **405,399**
Korean War = **36,516**
Vietnam War = **58,209**
Gulf War = **294**

It seems America was misled by journalistic factoids and media corporate conformity meant to inflame a "perceived" *Misery Index* "caused" by President Bush himself. Fact-checked numbers illuminate truth untold.

In the Obama presidency through 2014, there were 1,681 US soldier deaths in Afghanistan in 62 months, averaging 27 fatalities per month. In 87 months under President George W. Bush, there were 630 US soldier deaths in Afghanistan, averaging 7 fatalities per month. [19]

In early 2009, the Obama administration authorized the implementation of the COIN (Counter-Insurgent) strategy, more focused on "winning hearts and minds" than winning a war, and over the next five years, the US death toll nearly tripled. **73%** of *all* US military deaths in Afghanistan have taken place since 2009. [20]

What is more striking, though, is **more** US soldiers have been *killed and wounded* during President Barack Obama's first term in office than former President George W. Bush's two terms. And the anti-war mainstream media that regularly counted the number of deaths in Iraq and Afghanistan under Bush, for the most part, has **kept silent** on the number of deaths and casualties that have resulted under Barak Hussein Obama's clouded leadership.

Under former President George W. Bush, 575 American soldiers died and fewer than 3,000 were wounded in Afghanistan. Under Obama, at least 1,405 soldiers have died and nearly 15,000 additional soldiers have been wounded, which means 70% of the deaths, and nearly 80% of the injuries in Afghanistan, have occurred through Obama's repugnance of American might. [21]

Obama has presided over the top three deadliest years of the war in Afghanistan: 2009 (303 deaths); 2010 (497 deaths); and 2011 (399). Under Bush, fatalities peaked at 151 for the year 2008.[22] The superlative results of the War on Terror are rarely heard or factually laid out. Just in the early years of the war up to 2007 under President Bush, over 5,000 known terrorists were captured or killed by the US military, FBI, and CIA, which is the major reason why America has not been attacked again since 2001.

Thanks to improved interworking relationships between the CIA and FBI under Bush's leadership, American law enforcement has stopped 53 terrorist attack-plots in NY City alone since 9/11/2001.

Here is what the War on Terror accomplished during the George W. Bush presidential administration 2001-2007:

- Over 4.5 million people have clean drinking water for the first time in centuries in Iraq.
- Over 400,000 kids have up to date immunizations.
- Over 1,500 schools have been renovated and ridded of the weapons that were stored there so education can occur.
- The port of Uhm Qasar was renovated so grain can be loaded off from ships faster.
- School attendance is up 80% from pre-war levels.
- Iraq had its first 2 billion barrel export of oil.
- Iraq now emits 2 times the electrical power it did before the war.
- 100% of the hospitals are open and fully staffed compared to 35% before the war.
- Elections are taking place in every major city and city councils are in place.
- Sewer and water lines are installed in every major city.
- Over 60,000 police patrol the streets.
- Over 10,000 Iraqi defense police secure the country.
- Over 80,000 Iraqi soldiers patrol the borders.
- Over 400,000 have telephones for the first time.
- Students are taught field sanitation and hand-washing techniques to prevent the spread of germs.
- An Iraqi Constitution has been signed.
- Girls are allowed to attend school for the first time ever in Iraq.
- Text books that do not mention Saddam are in school for the first time in 30 years.

Khalid Sheikh Mohammed was born in Pakistan in 1964, grew up in Kuwait, joined the Muslim Brotherhood at age 16, then graduated from high school in 1983. He traveled to America to attend college at Chowan University, Murfreesboro, NC, later transferring to NC Agricultural State University to graduate with a BS in Mechanical Engineering.

Fast forward.

Khalid landed in the top 5 FBI's Most Wanted terrorists immediately following 9/11. Khalid was the "brains" and master-planner behind the 9/11/2001 Islamic terrorist attack that killed over 3,000 people, mostly American citizens.

A principal architect of international terror for al Qaeda, Khalid worked as the #2 leader under bin Laden behind the scenes.

Captured March 1, 2003, in Rawalpindi, a military garrison town southwest of the capital Islamabad, Pakistan, Khalid resided at 18a Nisar Road in the wealthy Westridge district of Rawalpind, a house owned by a prominent family suspected of having links to al Qaeda. The successful joint effort of the CIA and Pakistani's Counterterrorism Center led a raid met with minimal resistance from Khalid and his family.

While being held at Guantanamo Bay detention camp, in March 2007, Khalid confessed to masterminding the September 11, 2001, attacks, and confessed to being the author of at least 31 global terrorist plots, including:

- Richard Reid shoe bombing attempt to blow up an airliner (2001)
- Bali nightclub bombing in Indonesia (2002)
- 1993 World Trade Center bombing
- Executioner of *Wall Street Journal* reporter Daniel Pearl (2002)

Khalid was promptly charged in February 2008 with war crimes and murder by a US military commission at Guantanamo Bay detention camp in 2008. The 2008 charges included 2,973 individual counts of murder - one for each person killed in the 9/11 attacks. According to testimony by Attorney Philip Zelikow, Osama bin Laden was motivated by a desire to punish the US for supporting Israel and wanted to move up the attack date. Khalid argued for ensuring the teams were prepared, stating,

"[Bin Laden] allegedly told KSM it would be sufficient simply to down the planes and not hit specific targets. KSM stood his ground, arguing that the operation would not be successful unless the pilots were fully trained and the hijacking teams were larger." [23]

Osama thought any attack on American soil would serve as a recruiting bonanza for al Qaeda.

In court hearings, Khalid chided President Bush's "crusade war" and questioned the judge, alleging his bias at the 2008 trial, *"If you were part of Jerry Falwell or Pat Robertson's group, then you would not be impartial."* [24]

According to "unclassified summary of evidence" presented during Khalid's military tribunal hearing, a computer hard drive seized during the capture of Khalid Sheikh Mohammed contained incriminating photos, plans, pilot licenses, passports, and letters from Osama bin Laden.

In an attempt to publicly shame the Bush administration over the quagmired War on Terror in Iraq, *CNN* and *Time* magazine both reported in 2006 that Khalid confessed under brutal CIA "torture" and interrogation that he personally committed the murder of journalist Daniel Pearl. Thus, implying a false confession.

The Pentagon disagreed, documenting on March 15, 2007, Khalid confessed to the murder. The statement quoted Mohammed as saying, *"I decapitated with my blessed right hand the head of the American Jew, Daniel Pearl, in the city of Karachi, Pakistan. For those who would like to confirm, there are pictures of me on the internet holding his head."* [25]

In addition, an investigative report published in January 2011 by Georgetown University, the Federal Bureau of Investigation used vein matching to determine that the perpetrator in the video of the killing of Pearl was most likely Khalid, notably through identifying a "bulging vein" running across his hand.

Under new Presidential management in 2009, Obama's Attorney General, Eric Holder, announced the transfer of Khalid's case to a *civilian* court in New York, which angered New Yorkers and insulted 9/11 victim families. In 2010, pressure from the White House got all *military* charges dropped without prejudice against Khalid – calling it a "procedural move", so that Khalid's case could be tried in a civilian court in New York.

A Republican-led US Congress acted accordingly, passing the **Ike Skelton National Defense Authorization Act for Fiscal Year 2011**. Congress essentially prohibited the use of Pentagon funds to build facilities in the United States to house detainees, as Obama had originally proposed. The move essentially barred the administration from trying detainees in civilian courts in the US. Obama signed the law "kickin-n-screamin" vowing to appeal the restrictions.

Eric Holder ludicrously claimed the restrictions passed responsibly by Congress "harm" America's national security.

Seeing their original plans fail, Obama via Holder announced that Khalid Sheikh Mohammed and four other 9/11 terror suspects would face a military trial at the Guantanamo Bay detention facility. Holder strongly criticized Congress for imposing restrictions on the Justice Department's ability to bring the 9/11 attackers to New York for civilian trials.

Though the trial started May 2012 with Holder "promising" to seek the death penalty for each of the five men, on April 4 he warned it was an "open question" if such a penalty can be imposed by a military commission if the defendants plead guilty. Hint, hint.

A small group of 9/11 victim's families attended the first hearing. Khalid represented himself and protested by refusing to answer the judge's questions, refusing to enter a plea, labeling the trial impartial and unfair.

The most important terrorism trial in US history at the writing of this book still hasn't happened being muddled down in years of preliminary litigation. Arguments over issues like the mental competence of Khalid's codefendant Ramzi Binalshibh, and such nonstop shenanigans have backed up the start of the trial to 2016-17.

When the 800-page Senate *9/11 Commission Report* was made public in 2002, US Congressmen in both parties were shocked to see an important chapter (28 pages) in the report had been redacted (removed) beginning on page 395, detailing a role of foreign governments (namely Saudi Arabia) in bankrolling the 9/11 hijackers.

At the writing of this book, a federal judge in Sarasota, FL, is reviewing 80,000 pages of documents that relate to a prominent Saudi family and their extensive contacts with three of the hijackers when they attended flight school in Sarasota.

Attorney Jack Quinn, who previously represented families in the Lockerbie plane crash in their suit against the Libyan government, is representing 9/11 victim families in their effort to likewise gain long overdue compensation from the Saudi government.

Even Democrat Senator Bob Graham notes, *"both al Qaeda and ISIS are a creation of Saudi Arabia."* [27] Yet, the redacted documents of the 9/11 report have stayed secret for over a dozen years, fueling conspiracy theories that can only be put to rest by its release.

A Republican-led US Senate passed JASTA in 2014 (Justice Against Sponsors of Terrorism Act). Co-sponsored by Democrats and Republicans, the bill would strip diplomatic immunity from nation states in cases of terrorism, and open the door to financial compensation for the 9/11 families from the Saudi government. President Obama threatened the bill with a promised veto.

US Presidents Clinton, Bush, Obama:

43rd United States President George W. Bush:

Khalid Sheikh Mohammed trial:

I've had a few close shaves with the CIA

1999 Clinton cable to Iran:

Chapter Seven

Deaths of Saddam Hussein and Osama bin Laden

*Our enemies have made the mistake that America's enemies
always make. They saw liberty and thought they saw weakness,
and now, they see defeat.*[1]

George W. Bush

43rd President of the United States

Let's roll![2]

Todd Beamer

UA Flight 93 passenger
Battle cry in an attempt to retake the plane from terrorists

Saddam Hussein:

Operation Red Dawn (coined after 1984 movie, *Red Dawn*) was a mission assigned to the 1st Brigade Combat Team of the 4th Infantry Division, commanded by Maj. Gen. Raymond Odierno and led by Col. James Hickey on 12/13/2003 in ad-Dawr, Iraq, which led to the capture of Iraq's brutal President from 1979-2003, Saddam Hussein.

Eight months after being ousted from power, a lengthy investigation involving Saddam's family members and bodyguards by intelligence officers were able to determine his general location.

Originally tasked with searching two sites, "Wolverine 1" and "Wolverine 2," on the outskirts of ad-Dawr, they did not locate Saddam. A continued search between the two sites found Saddam near a farmhouse holed up in an underground foxhole 6-8 ft deep called a "spider hole." Though Saddam had with him (2) AK-47 rifles and $750,000 in $100 bills, he did not resist capture.

President George W. Bush announced shortly thereafter to the Iraqi nation, *"You do not have to fear the rule of Saddam Hussein ever again.. [Saddam will] face the justice he denied to millions. For the *Ba'athist holdouts responsible for the violence, there will be no return to the corrupt power and privilege they once held."*
* Ba'ath = Arab **Socialist** Party

Five months earlier, Saddam's two sons, Uday and Qusay, met their well-deserved fate in a gun battle against US military forces.

The scions of Saddam were monsters to the core.

The eldest, Uday, was widely feared with a reputation for ordering any girl or woman who caught his eye to be brought to his private "pleasure dome" at the Presidential palace, raping girls as young as twelve. Uday's entourage would pass by a wedding reception; stop in to literally crash the party by forcing the bride to have sex with him under bodyguard protection.

With a penchant for fast cars, loud and drunken parties, expensive suits and flowing robes; murder, rape, and torture, were a part of Uday's sadistic thrill ride. Lest we soon forget, this is socialism's political power unchained.

In a cruel and ruthless lack of discipline, Uday bludgeoned and stabbed to death one of Saddam's favorite bodyguards at a 1988 party. Saddam briefly had him imprisoned and beaten. This caused Saddam to begin favoring his second son, Qusay.

Overseer of Iraq's Olympic Committee and national football (soccer) team, Uday would call the locker room during half-time to threaten to cut off players' legs and throw them to ravenous dogs. Uday was known to keep a private torture scorecard with written instructions on how many times each player should be beaten on the soles of his feet after a particularly poor showing.

Uday is also reported to have operated an even more private torture chamber on the banks of the Tigris River, studying more severe techniques of torture craft.

After a 1996 failed assassination attempt on Uday's life in a blaze of gunfire striking his red Porsche (1 of 100 cars) as he sped through the streets of Baghdad, some speculate the extreme back pain Uday lived with for the rest of his life due to bullet wounds contributed to his cruelty. Yet, the murders, shooting, and erratic behavior put him in permanent outs with Saddam.

At the start of America's War on Terror, the US government posted a $15 million reward for information leading to the discovery of all 3 Hussein men's location.

An informant's tip led US Special Forces to a house in which they were both staying on July 22, 2003, in a northern Iraqi city of Mosul. After drawing fire, the US soldiers withdrew, until receiving backup in the form of 100 troops from the 101st Airborne division, Apache helicopters, and an A-10 gunship. Following a hail of gunfire and missile strikes, Americans entered the house and found bodies of the two Hussein brothers dead, as well as Qusay's 14 year old son. They were buried in a cemetery near the city of Tikrit, Iraq.

Left-leaning American media just couldn't help themselves to belittle this incredible victory in the wake of their deaths, foaming criticism of the Bush-led war effort for releasing photos of Uday and Qusay's lifeless bodies on a gurney. US Government officials clarified the move was necessary to convince the skeptical Iraqi people that the long-feared brothers were truly dead.

Let's rewind a bit.

Saddam originally sparked an international crisis in 1990 when Iraq attacked the sovereign country of Kuwait, claiming to be assisting "Kuwaiti revolutionaries." It was described as Saddam doing exactly what his Gulf neighbors were paying him to prevent – all in the name of Islam and Arab nationalism.

On August 8, 1990, Saddam announced a "merger" of the two nations, believing Kuwait was an original 19th province of Iraq.

Then US President George H.W. Bush cautiously collaborated with the Soviet Union to seek passage of resolutions from the National Security Council giving Saddam a deadline to leave Kuwait or face military extraction. Saddam called Bush's bluff to his own peril.

The **Persian Gulf War** was a coalition of 34 nations led by the US conducting **Operation Desert Storm** (Aug. 1990 – Jan. 1991) and **Operation Desert Shield** (Jan. 1991 – Feb. 1991) to remove Iraq from Kuwait. Labeled a "quick and easy" war, the Iraq forces mostly surrendered being superiorly outnumbered and unable to compete with overpowering air support and highly adept mobile land forces.

Some 175,000 Iraqi soldiers were taken prisoners of war with around 85,000 casualties. A cease-fire agreement was conditioned upon Iraq's ending all germ weapons and poison gas, allow UN inspectors to observe all sites, and UN trade sanctions were implemented. Saddam publicly declared victory.

A belligerent Saddam seemed to defy the world. US officials constantly accused Saddam of violating terms of the Gulf War's cease fire, by developing weapons of mass destruction and other banned weaponry, thus also violating UN-imposed sanctions. President Bill Clinton maintained sanctions and ordered ineffective air strikes in the "Iraqi no-fly zones" (**Operation Desert Fox**).

A 2000 video shows Saddam "cozying up" to al-Jazeera's managing director, Mohammed Jassem al-Ali, a Muslim brotherhood advocate. It soon became apparent that not only was Saddam covertly defying sanctions, but Iraq was functioning as a safe-harbor for known terrorists, and was a central hub for sponsoring terrorist activities around the globe.

Then 9/11/2001 happened.

After Saddam's capture in 2003, Saddam was interrogated by FBI agent George Piro. The guards at the Baghdad detention facility, where Saddam spent his final days, called their prisoner "Vic." He was allowed to plant a small garden near his cell. Saddam also kept a journal.

In June 2004, Saddam was handed over to the interim Iraqi government to stand trial for crimes against humanity. Specific charges include the murder of 148 people, torture of women and children, as well as 399 illegal arrests.

On November 5, 2006, Saddam was found guilty along with 11 other Ba'athist leaders, including Saddam's half brother, all sentenced to death by hanging. Saddam's request to be executed by gunshot was denied. The execution was carried out at Camp Justice, an Iraqi army base in Kadhimiya, a neighborhood northeast of Baghdad on December 6, 2006.

Online cell phone videos of Saddam's hanging released by Iraqi nationals sparked an outcry from progressive human rights groups. Even more, it was later claimed by a head guard overseeing Saddam's burial that his body was stabbed 6 times after hanging.

Saddam was interred at his birthplace, Al-Awja in Tikrit, Iraq.

Osama bin Laden:

In bizarre admission, Wakil Ahmad Muttawakil, Taliban's former foreign minister in Afghanistan, told *Al Jazeera TV* network in an exclusive 2011 interview that his government had made several proposals to the United States in 2001 to hand over al-Qaeda leader, Osama bin Laden.

One such proposal was to set up a three-nation court, or something similar, under the supervision of the Organization of the Islamic Conference. Of course, the US wisely showed no interest, because the US did not recognize a Taliban government and had no direct diplomatic relations with the group which controlled most of Afghanistan between 1996 and 2001.

According to Muttawakil, there had always been differences of opinion between the Arab fighters of al-Qaeda and his Taliban colleagues. When 9/11 occurred, the Taliban government immediately convened an advisory gathering of over 1,500 religious scholars at a Kabul hotel to discuss what to do with bin Laden. The scholars concluded that the Taliban government should ask bin Laden to "leave the country voluntarily." Osama did leave and found his native Saudi Arabia had also revoked his citizenship.

Another idea floated by Muttawakil was that Osama would be brought to trial before a group of Ulema (religious scholars) in Afghanistan. Yet, no one in the US government took these offers seriously because they did not trust the Taliban nor their ability to conduct a proper trial.

Muttawakil contends that Afghanistan was one of the first countries to officially condemn the 9/11 attacks, knowing the reprisals soon to come to the Afghan country, as well as to the Taliban, and knowing the US would decisively act seeking justice.

A mobile Osama would taunt the United States for over 10 years after 9/11/2001 with no less than 31 audio or video recordings promising more future terrorist attacks.

It was a (yet unnamed) female CIA agent working (often without support from her CIA colleagues) for years in Langley, VA, who ultimately tracked Osama bin Laden's location. Through persistent pressure, it was an idea from this CIA spy, a "targeter," to covertly hawk mail delivery assistants (couriers), until Osama's courier led them to his hide-a-way in Pakistan. Here's how it happened..

Dr. Shakil Afridi graduated from Khyber Medical College in Peshawar in 1990. He went on to serve as a senior health official of Khyber Pakhtunkhwa Province, along the mountainous Afghan border in Pakistan.

In late 2009, Afridi attended a seminar on children's health issues hosted by *Save the Children* and *USAID* (United States Agency for International Development). Afridi claims to have been recruited by the CIA through *USAID* to employ a Hepatitis B vaccine program in the region.

At the same time, a disgruntled former Pakistani army officer had tipped off the CIA that a prominent al Qaeda militant "might" be living behind the 20 ft. towering walls of the "Waziristan Kothi" (the Waziristan Apartment), situated in a well-to-do suburb of Bilal Town. Pakistani villagers rumored the residents of the compound to be out-of-towner families escaping a tribal feud, who preferred to keep to themselves.

The CIA ploy of staging a vaccination campaign to gain entry into the compound would work if the discarded needles of bin Laden's children were handed over to the CIA for a DNA match to Osama. This would substantiate cause for a raid.

The Pakistani military would shoot down any US helicopters or attack Navy SEALs on the ground launching a raid. The possibility of a bombing run was ruled out because collecting a DNA sample from the rubble to identify that bin Laden had been killed would be practically impossible.

When Afridi and a health worker arrived at the Waziristan Kothi, a woman answering the gate refused him entrance stating that none of the residents were home. Afridi asked to speak with the owner of the house to no avail, but was able to obtain a phone number belonging to "Ibrahim Saeed Ahmed," a courier who assisted the compound. The CIA knew Ibrahim as bin Laden's trusted courier.

Green light.

The raid was planned by joint operations of the CIA and the US Navy's JSOC (Joint Special Operations Command) January 2011 under the leadership of Vice Admiral William H. McRaven. President Obama met with the National Security Council to review 14 different options. Obama ruled out involving the Pakistanis, because he wanted the mission to proceed quickly and was originally leaning toward a bombing mission.

The bombing mission was ruled out for good reasons: 1) the compound may have an underground bunker, 2) it would be almost impossible to find and collect a DNA sample of Osama to confirm the kill. McRaven then presented a helicopter raid.

A SEAL team performed rehearsals of the raid in two locations in the US around April 10: 1) at Harvey Point Defense Testing Activity facility in North Carolina where a 1:1 version of bin Laden's compound was built, and 2) in Nevada on April 18. The Nevada training simulated the 4,000 elevation altitude of Osama's compound to see the effect it may have on the helicopter.

The plan was if Osama surrendered, he would be held near Bagram Air Base in Afghanistan. If the SEALs were discovered by the Pakistanis in the middle of the raid, Joint Chiefs Chairman Admiral Mike Mullen would call Pakistan's army chief General Ashfaq Parvez Kayani and try to negotiate their release. When the National Security Council (NSC) met again on April 19, Obama gave provisional approval for the helicopter raid. Only Vice President Joe Biden completely opposed it.

SEAL Team Six departed the US from Naval Air Station Oceana on April 26 in a C-17 aircraft, refueled on the ground at Ramstein Air Base in Germany, landed at Bagram Air Base, then moved to Jalalabad on April 27. McRaven and the SEALs left for Afghanistan to practice at a one-acre, full-scale replica of the compound built on a restricted area of Bagram known as Camp Alpha.

On April 30, Obama placed a final call to McRaven to wish the SEALs well and to thank them for their service. The same evening, was the White House Correspondents Association dinner, attended by Obama, hosted by comedian Seth Meyers. At one point, Meyers jokes: *"People think bin Laden is hiding in the Hindu Kush, but did you know that every day from 4 to 5 he hosts a show on C-SPAN?"* Obama laughed.

Twelve Chinook military helicopters were kept on standby in a deserted area roughly two-thirds of the way from Jalalabad to Abbottabad, with two additional SEAL teams consisting of approximately 24 SEAL operators. Their mission was to intercept any interference with the raid. More Chinooks, holding 25 more SEALs, were stationed just across the border in Afghanistan in case reinforcements were needed during the raid.

To enter Pakistan "low to the ground and undetected" the raid was scheduled for a time with little moonlight. The helicopters used hillside terrain and nap-of-the-earth techniques to reach the compound without appearing on any radar nor alerting the Pakistani military. The flight from Jalalabad to Abbottabad took about 90 minutes.

The mission sent in the first helicopter hovering over the compound yard, while its full team of SEALs fast-roped to the ground. At the same time, the second helicopter would fly to the northeast corner of the compound and deploy the interpreter, the dog and handler, and four SEALs to secure the perimeter. The team in the courtyard was to enter the house from the ground floor.

The raid was planned to take all of 40 minutes. From entry of the compound to exit took SEAL Team Six 38 minutes. The military offensive aspect of the raid took 15 minutes.

Two of Osama's men lived on first floor of the compound, Osama and his family lived on the 2nd and 3rd floors, which were the last to be cleared.

Just after midnight on **May 2, 2011**, a 40-man Navy squadron (SEAL Team Six) equipped with NVGs (Night Vision Goggles) raided the compound in Abbottabad, Pakistan, killing al Qaeda leader Osama bin Laden with bullets to the head, simply because US President Obama followed former US President George W. Bush's policy on the War on Terror, ending a ten-year manhunt in just under 40 minutes.

Our utmost pride and thanks goes out to the operators of **Operation Neptune Spear**.

A military dog, Cairo, a Belgian Malinois, was used to track hidden rooms or doors, and guard the perimeter from escapees.

A wife of Osama called out his name during the raid, inadvertently assisting in his identification for SEAL Team members. Osama used one of his wives as a human shield. Three other men, and a woman, were killed in the raid: Osama's adult son, Osama's courier, the courier's brother and his wife.

One of the two "stealth" version Black Hawk helicopters developed a hazardous airflow condition, known as "vortex ring state" and had to make a hard landing into the compound wall, due to higher than expected temperatures. The tail grazed the wall and rolled to its side, as the pilot stuck the nose into the ground to avoid tipping over. It was a soft crash landing with no fatalities nor serious injuries. The SEAL Team destroyed all sensitive information inside the helicopter before exiting the premises.

A brief firefight took place on the ground on the first level where the first man was killed. Another man and his wife encountered the team on floor one and were killed. Osama's son challenged the SEAL Team on stairs going up to the upper floors and was killed.

The SEALs first encountered Osama on the third floor of the main building. Osama was "wearing the local loose-fitting tunic and pants known as a kurta paijama," which were later found to have 500 euros and two phone numbers stitched into the fabric. Osama peered through his bedroom door at the SEALs advancing up the stairs, and then retreated into the room as the lead SEAL fired a shot at him, which either missed or hit him in the side. Navy SEAL **Robert O'Neill**, who later publicly identified himself as the SEAL who shot Osama bin Laden, rolled through the door and confronted Osama inside the bedroom. In Seymour Hersh's online reports, Osama was found cowering and shot dead:
lrb.co.uk/v37/n10/seymour-m-hersh/the-killing-of-osama-bin-laden

US intelligence reports put 22 people in the compound with five killed, including Osama bin Laden. An unnamed Pakistani security official claimed one of bin Laden's daughters told Pakistani investigators that Osama was captured alive, then in front of family members was shot dead by American forces and dragged to a helicopter.

Osama's photograph was transmitted by the SEALs to CIA headquarters in Langley, Virginia, for facial recognition analysis, which yielded a 90-95 percent match. One or two women from the compound, including one of Osama's wives, identified Osama's body. A military medic took bone marrow samples for DNA matching, which was positively identified in Afghanistan by comparison to Osama's sister's DNA who died of brain cancer.

Within 24 hours of his death, US military officials announced that after the raid, US forces took bin Laden's body to Afghanistan for identification, then buried him at sea in accordance with Islamic tradition.

The body of Osama bin Laden was flown from Bagram, Afghanistan, to aircraft carrier USS Carl Vinson in a V-22 Osprey tilt rotor helicopter escorted by two US Navy F/A-18 fighter jets. According to US officials, bin Laden was buried at sea because no country would accept his remains, and so that his tomb would not be made a shrine. Before disposing of the body, the US called the Saudi government, who approved of burying the body in the ocean. Muslim religious rites were performed aboard the USS Carl Vinson in the North Arabian Sea within 24 hours of bin Laden's death. [3]

The body was washed, wrapped in a white sheet and placed in a weighted plastic bag. An officer read prepared religious remarks which were translated into Arabic by a native speaker. Afterward, bin Laden's body was placed onto a flat board. The board was tilted upward on one side and the body slid off into the sea. In *Worthy Fights: A Memoir of Leadership in War and Peace*, Defense Secretary Leon Panetta wrote that bin Laden's body was draped in a white shroud, given final prayers in Arabic and placed inside a black bag loaded with heavy metals of 300 pounds of iron chains inside apparently to ensure that it would sink and never float. The body bag was placed on a white table at the rail of the ship, and the table was tipped to let the body bag slide into the sea, but the body bag did not slide and took the table with it. The table bobbed on the surface while the weighted body sank into the depths. [4]

At 11:35pm ET, President Obama appeared on all major TV networks to publicly announce the death of Osama bin Laden.

Controversy brewed by *Amnesty International* over the decision to not release any photographic or DNA evidence of bin Laden's death to the public.

The Navy SEAL who shot and killed Osama bin Laden, Ron O'Neill, also plays a supporting Navy SEAL role in blockbuster movie hits *American Sniper* and *Captain Phillips*. See Ryan's interview online, as he talks about the night he killed Osama bin Laden:
dailycaller.com/2014/10/29/fox-news-lands-interview-with-seal-member-that-killed-osama-bin-laden/

The raid was supported by 9 out of 10 Americans surveyed by a Gallup poll on 5/3/2011.[5] Osama's death was welcomed by the United Nations, NATO, the European Union, and a lengthy list of world governments.

It was reported in a Kuwaiti newspaper May 2011 that Osama bin Laden had left a will written a short time after the September 11, 2001, attacks in which he urged his children **not to join al Qaeda** and **not to continue holy war jihad**.[6]

Osama is survived by around 14 children and $30M he inherited from his father, who owned a successful Saudi construction company.

While Americans were celebrating the next day, Pakistani officials and generals were fuming. They were more embarrassed than anything to not know bin Laden was living right under their noses, while their own spy network (ISI) was oblivious to it.

ISI agents began arresting and interrogating anyone near the Waziristan Kothi in recent days. Dr. Afridi, who assisted the CIA in the original covert vaccine program that located Osama, was arrested 3 weeks after the raid by Pakistani authorities.

In July 2011, acting CIA Director Michael Morell and ISI Chief Lieutenant General Ahmed Shuja Pasha discussed releasing Afridi, but no agreement was reached. In May 2012, a Pakistani tribal court decided not to charge Afridi with treason and instead fined him $3,100 and sentenced him to 33 years in prison.

In Washington, Republicans have been vocal in criticizing Pakistan's treatment of Dr. Afridi. At a congressional hearing on US foreign assistance April 2014, Republicans questioned US funding for Pakistan, which amounts to $882 million annually.

US Congressman Dana Rohrabacher (R-CA) reiterated to members of the House Committee on Foreign Affairs, *"Pakistan arrested and is still holding and brutalizing Dr. Afridi, who helped us identify and locate Osama bin Laden, who was responsible for slaughtering 3,000 Americans."* [7]

Representative Rohrabacher asked President Obama to intercede on Afridi's behalf, introducing two bills, H.R. 4069 to award a Congressional Gold Medal to Dr. Afridi, and H.R. 3901 to declare Afridi a naturalized US citizen. Obama did nothing with the opportunities, and both bills were sent to subcommittees, where they have languished since 2012.

The US Senate Appropriations Committee cut $33 million in aid to Pakistan in May 2012 over the conviction of Afridi: $1 million for each of the 33 years of Afridi's sentence. Pakistan receives almost a billion dollars in military and economic aid annually from the US for being a schizophrenic ally.

In November 2012, Dr. Afridi went on a hunger strike protesting his solitary confinement and prison conditions.

In June 2013, Pakistani regional officials lifted a ban on relatives and lawyers to visit Afridi. The surprise move came after US Special Envoy for Afghanistan and Pakistan, James Dobbin, met with Pakistani leaders.

The 33 year prison sentence of Dr. Afridi was overturned in August 2013, and a retrial was ordered. Government administrator Feroz Shah said a senior judicial official, Sahibzada Mohammad Anis, issued the ruling because the person who originally sentenced Dr. Afridi was not authorized to hear the case.

Dr. Afridi can't seem to catch a break. He remains jailed on what has been described as a "bizarre" murder charge: being blamed for the death of a teenage boy in 2005, weeks after Afridi performed an appendicitis surgery. The mother blames Afridi for the death of her son, perhaps to play along with the societal spite hurled against him.

In May 2015, investigative journalist Sy Hersh interviewed a retired CIA official anonymously. In Hersh's interview, the retired CIA official identified Dr. Afridi as a scapegoat delivered by the CIA and State Department to take the fallout brunt from Pakistan.

Afridi, who helped the CIA track a mastermind terrorist, has received little help from the US after his crucial role in locating Osama bin Laden.

His own countrymen count Afridi as part of a Western plot "vaccination scheme" to sterilize all Pakistani Muslims. He last communicated with the outside world in September 2012, calling *Fox News* on a cell phone that had been smuggled into his cell. Three prison officials and guards were severely punished thereafter.

Afridi's supporters appear to have abandoned him at home and abroad, including his alleged US supporters within the CIA and the Obama administration. His Facebook page "**Free Dr. Shakil Alfridi NOW**" had 430 likes at the writing of this book. View **freeafridi.com** for current updates.

In his native Pakistan, Dr. Shakil Afridi is considered a traitor by many people for helping the Central Intelligence Agency track down and kill Osama bin Laden. In the United States, he is hailed as a hero.

Today, Afridi is still in solitary confinement at Peshawar Central Prison, a fortified red-brick remnant of Britain's colonial rule that is crammed with more than 2,000 inmates, ranging from petty thieves to Taliban assassins.

In 2013, *WikiLeaks* released documents bolstering the claim that Osama bin Laden was not buried at sea at all.

According to Statfor emails, an intelligence and geopolitical analysis company, hacked by Anonymous LulzSec and received by *WikiLeaks* in December 2012, a tale of misdirection emerges.

Though Statfor is not officially associated with the US Government, their stolen data comprises 2.7 million company emails, along with other private information of Stratfor readers, subscribers and employees.

Statfor's vice-president for intelligence, Fred Burton, surmised from emails that Osama's body was bound for Dover, Delaware, on a CIA plane after his capture, then onward to the Armed Forces Institute of Pathology in Bethesda, Maryland.

Sure to stoke conspiracy theorists, Burton says some emails may have been forged, others may be authentic.

Two major movie trailers detailing CIA and military aspects of **Operation Neptune Spear** were curiously released around the same time just weeks prior to the 2012 reelection of President Barak Hussein Obama. *Vanity Fair* magazine arrogantly coined the movies Obama's "October surprise".

Zero Dark Thirty and *SEAL Team Six: The Raid on Osama bin Laden* were both set to premier on the big screen and television in October 2012, which conservative critics correctly labeled as a $30 million "political ad campaign" for Obama, who campaigned with chest-pounding the al Qaeda leader was assassinated on his watch.

Then, national suspicion arose when *NY Times* columnist, Maureen Dowd, pointed out that *Zero Dark Thirty* producers Kathryn Bigelow and Mark Boal gained unusual top-level access to classified mission intel from the Obama administration. The White House appeared to have outsourced the job of manning-up Obama's image through Hollywood sympathizers.

White House spokespersons flatly denied any "speculation" of Obama's authorization, yea approval, of any assistance to a movie production about the most important military mission of the new millennium. Yet, words are cheap in liberal-led government.

Conservative legal group *Judicial Watch* shortly thereafter obtained 300 pages of legal documents through the **Freedom of Information Act** detailing special access Bigelow and Boal received to produce their Obama-propping movie. Republican Representative Peter King (NY), chairman of the House of Representatives Committee on Homeland Security, responsibly called for an immediate investigation into the White House's manipulative role to facilitate Bigelow's movie.

King's committee substantiated documentation in late May 2012 of an email from Michael Vickers, an Undersecretary of Defense for Intelligence, who was interviewed by Bigelow and Boal, explaining that he helped the filmmakers at the behest of Obama's Secretary of Defense and former CIA director Leon Panetta.

Though Obama's Pentagon and CIA both repeatedly denied the filmmakers saw anything classified, they pivoted 180° to defend the special access granted when factual documents showed otherwise, saying, they were hoping to "prevent gross inaccuracies" in the movie. Uh-huh.

Zero Dark Thirty's official release date was pushed back until after the November 2 elections to mid December, thanks to the valiant patriotic pressure exerted daily by minute-men conservatives on *Fox News* and talk radio exposing the movie's dubious intention to sway a national election.

Ginning up support from leftists everywhere, it was oddly out of character for so many *liberals* to be seen "praising" a war movie. Or, was it the war movie they were actually praising?

The Obama campaign still benefitted from TV film *SEAL Team Six: The Raid on Osama bin Laden*, produced by Obama supporter Harvey Weinstein and broadcast on the *National Geographic Channel* **two days before his reelection.** *Zero Dark Thirty* trailer was released 3 months before voters went to the voting booth. Obama's reelection fits in tandem with a 93% Gallup approval poll asking Americans how they felt about the mission which killed Osama bin Laden.[8]

It was noted that the Obama Administration seemingly rolled out the red carpet for filmmakers akin to political oneness, but worked to limit access by independent journalists to information about the May 2011 raid. Conservative Republicans opined that the filmmakers received access to classified information -- all in an effort to ensure the Obama White House was painted in the most favorable light during the reelection of Obama in 2012.

According to relatives of Betty Ong, an AA Flight 11 attendant, a clip from her recorded final call to headquarters was used in the beginning of *Zero Dark Thirty* without attribution. Mary and Frank Fetchet, parents of Brad Fetchet, who worked on the 89th floor of the World Trade Center South Tower, also rebuked filmmakers Bigelow and Boals for using a recording of their son's voicemail without permission.

In June 2013, an unreleased IG report from the US Defense Department Inspector General's office stated that former CIA Director Leon Panetta, while giving a presentation at a private awards ceremony, disclosed information classified as "Top Secret" regarding personnel involved in the raid on the bin Laden compound. "Unbeknownst" to Panetta, screenwriter Mark Boal was among the 1,300 present during the ceremony. [9]

Zero Dark Thirty made $132M at the box office on a budget of $40M winning several nominations in various categories at the 2013 Academy Awards and Golden Globe Awards.

Both movies ultimately served as a clear vindication of the previous Bush administration's War on Terror policy to kill with prejudice all known anti-American terrorists.

The Iraqi Judge who sentenced Saddam Hussein to death was captured and executed by ISIS forces, as US President Obama did little to prevent ISIS terrorists from retaking Iraq. On June 16, 2014, Rauf Rashid was arrested by ISIS rebels during a 2014 Northern Iraq offensive and executed "in retaliation for the death of the martyr Saddam Hussein." [10]

Saddam Hussein:

Operation Red Dawn:

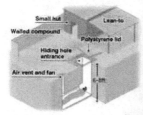

Uday and Qusay Hussein:

Osama bin laden (Operation Neptune Spear):

 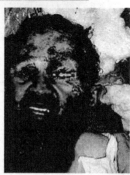

Osama bin Laden compound, the Waziristan Apartment, Bilal Town, Abbottabad, Pakistan:

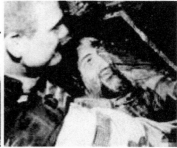

Armed Forces Institute of Pathology, Bethesda Maryland

USS Carl Vinson

Osama bin Laden killspot:

Iraqi Judge Rauf Rashid and Saddam Hussein:

Chapter Eight

9/11 Poems

I saw a terrible tragedy and yelled at God, 'How could you let
such a thing happen? Why didn't you do something!?'
A little while later, God's answer came:
'I did do something. I made you.' [1]

Kevin Mills
September 11th Memorial Service
9/9/2005

In a New York classroom one year following 9/11/2001, students composed the following 9/11 poem. A relative of the teacher perished in Tower One of the World Trade Center. The victim left behind a 3-year-old child. This poem was written to honor 9/11 victims:

List of "Don't Forgets" and "Remembers"

We were eight.

Before September 11, we'd wake up with a list of "Don't Forgets"
Don't forget to wash your face
Don't forget to brush your teeth
Don't forget to do your homework
Don't forget to wear your jacket
Don't forget to clean your room
Don't forget to take a bath

After September 11th, we wake up with a list of "Remembers"
Remember to greet the sun each morning
Remember to enjoy every meal
Remember to thank your parents for their hard work
Remember to honor those who keep you safe
Remember to value each person you meet
Remember to respect other's beliefs

Now we are nine. [2]

———————————

One month following the 9/11 attack, eleven-year-old Aaron Walsh wrote the following poem in his school notebook, trying to make sense of this horrible thing that had happened:

I Hold in My Hands
Aaron Walsh, 2001

I hold in my hands ...
The dust.
The dust and wreckage of the towers.
Even though I wasn't there,
I can still feel it.

It has damaged my hands with dirt.
It has damaged my heart with sorrow.
It has damaged my body with fear,
and it has damaged my life with war.

I hold in my hands ...
My life.
My life could soon be filled with war,
cruelty at its worst.
Miles away, I can hear the planes' roaring engines,
gliding through the air.

I hold in my hands ...
My future.
My life ahead.
Whether it will be filled with war or peace, we will not know.
My future keeps me going from dawn to dusk.

I hold in my hands ...
Hope.
Hope for the future.
Hope for peace.
Hope for my country's freedom.
And hope for America to win this war on terrorism. [3]

A student named Lindsay, from a school called Franklin Elementary, wrote this 9/11 poem.

September 11

On this day,
my heart crumbled,

On this day,
I really trembled.

Has the world changed in so many ways?
You know we have God to praise!

Ask Him for peace in your heart and mind,
you'll have comfort all the time! [4]

Hannah Schoechert's 9/11 poem, a 7th grade student:

We're Still Standing

Those twin towers
Standing tall with pride,
Fell with grieving hearts.
Stunned, America cried.

But we're still standing.

Bin Laden tried
To crush our land,
But we stood our ground
With our flag in hand.

And we're still standing.

Red for valor
And the blood that fell.
White for purity
Our heroes tell.
Blue for the justice
That will be done,
Proving once more
These colors don't run.

And we're still standing. [5]

If They Could Speak is a 9/11 poem written by Rosanne Pellicane in 2001. It was selected as keynote for the permanent 9/11 exhibit at the New York City Fire Museum. It honors the 343 firefighters who lost their lives at the World Trade Center.

If They Could Speak

Please don't be afraid.
Yes, life is different now, but remember, when it was beautiful?
Well, it will be again, though not the same.

The wounds will heal, your tears will dry and though scars remain,
I know you are strong enough to live through the pain.

Do not grieve and linger in the shadows of graves.
Go out into the sunshine and tell everyone that I was here.
Let our enemy know that when we were together we lived,
and worked and loved.
And though I am gone, you will carry on for me because you must.

Tell my family how much I loved them and still do.
Remember the good we shared, the life we created, and
walk forward with noble dreams.
God can't fill a shattered heart or a clenched fist.
Let fear die and let love flow again like a river.

So as the smoke rises high above the ash,
gather all your strength and rebuild something new, something better.
It's not impossible.
It's essential.
It's what I would do for you.

Just one last thing, surely you must know,
I never wanted to leave you.
I was captured by fate, escorted by angels.
And though you might feel you are alone,
you are not and neither am I ...

Love always. [6]

Written in 2001 from the vantage point of a 9/11 "survivor"
whose life was sparred,

WTC 9/11

Cristin O'Keefe Aptowicz

Lucky Kim, my roommate, is sleeping
next to me after 13 hours of solid television coverage.

She is the only person I have seen,
waking me up in the morning, asking:

"What are your plans for today,
because two planes just crashed
into the World Trade Center."

Lucky Kim, who works
at the World Financial Center,
stayed home today and got the news
between her morning run and cracking
open her books for study.

Together, we watched the news
and she points out her building attached to the towers
by gory amputated bridges, windows shattered, metal buckled.

And for hours,
we call her friends, coworkers:
Busy signals, no answers.

I run out for juice and donuts
and after that, we eat, drink and lean into each other,
in front of the tv.

We only have one channel now,
all the rest went down with the towers.
And the computers and telephones join the tv
in a parade of whirling ineffectiveness:

What's happening? What's happening?

Heads hungry for information,
we dumbly watch the plane bank
again and again into deadly blossom,
listen to the survivors,
watch the dust people run from the rumble,
our hands on the phone, waiting, waiting.

We watch.

All of lower Manhattan,
all of New York City,
consumed in this cloud:
dirt, paper, plaster, people. [7]

Silence (over Manhattan)
Paula Bardell, 2002

A black September shadow cloaks the dawn,
The City's once white teeth now rotting stumps,
Midst choking dusty embers ether-borne,
Its shrunken soundless heart now barely pumps.
Infernos upon retribution rise,
Fanaticism maddening the flames,
Its once imposing deities abscise,
As the faceless antagonist proclaims:
A consummation sweet but unfulfilled,
A penetrative burst without regret,
A zealous passion never to be stilled,
An earthly instinct powerful, and yet -
This bitter loathing blowing from the East,
Curtailed but could not kill the feisty beast. [8]

Tomorrow
Michael Brett

Tomorrow, it will all run backwards.

The steel tsunamis will froth back upwards
And become solid.
The planes will be pulled out like javelins
And slide backwards, swallowing their vapour trails.

Tomorrow, everyone will be fine.

Tomorrow, everyone who died will come home.
They will sit again at the tables of home
And rejoin life's fellowship, its snapshots, tea
And picnics.

Tomorrow, all will be well.

Everyone will sleep as babies do under mobiles,
Untroubled by strange sounds, of aero engines
Flying too low and shadows over the streets.

Tomorrow, mobile phones will be just toys again.
The sky will be clear, blue, unbroken. [9]

9/11 – Poem
David McLansky

They told us all 'to just stay put,
Breathing ashes and blackened soot,
'Put a towel against the door,
'Wet it first, put it on the floor;
'The Firemen were on the way,
That's what 911 said that day;
But I've always had an ornery streak,
When told to obey and to be meek,
We were told to wait in that fiery din;
'Be patient, the firemen were coming in;
But I rebelled; I could not sit still,
I would not cling to the windowsill,
I was tired of always following orders,
I had to think of my two daughters;
So for once I dared to rebel
To exit from that burning hell;
As in the fires of Serengeti,
In whirling smoke and wild confetti,
I held a towel to my face,
A savage in a human race;
Through the choking smoke and fire
Stumbling in the twisting gyre,
Blindly, pushing, through the smell
I made it to the South stairwell;
I joined a mob of screams and cries,
Of burnt white shirts and silken ties;
Of torn pants suits and sooted skirts,

The stairway lights flashing on alert;
Rebels all we descended
Heedless of whom we offended;
In the crowd a woman fell,
Who she was I could not tell,
Yet I stopped to help her up,
How odd she held a coffee cup;
Down and down we stumbled down,
A woman wore a wedding gown,
In the stink and smoke and fire,
Careless of our ruined attire,
We stumbled downward in our haste,
Our only thought to escape;
We met the firemen coming up,
Our downward flow slowed abrupt;
We let them pass, they let us pass,
Above we heard a roaring crash;
From above fell chunks of debris,
We ran downward one thought to flee;
But the firemen shoved us to run up,
Anger flared, some were cuffed;
We pushed downward amid the screams
We heard the wail of police sirens;
And suddenly I was in the lobby,
My knees were shaken, my steps were wobbly;
I was led away cut and bruised,
I realized I had lost my shoes;
I staggered barefoot up the street,
In a rain of paper sheets;
Whose files these were I didn't know,
But they all came down like scattered snow;
I was ushered on by waving cops,
'Head North! ' they shouted, I didn't stop
I saw a priest give a man extreme unction,
In the middle of a cross street junction;
I was alive, I had rebelled,
I walked Northward from that evil smell. [10]

Bravery of the Firefighters
Author Unknown

These thoughts combined in ev'ry mind
As watchers scanned the skies.
These doubts were asked as buildings basked
In wreaths of sure demise.
The heart went faint who tried to paint
A picture of the fate,
Of those who tried to stem the tide
Before it was too late.

Into the throes with heavy clothes
Those firefighters walked.
They made no press to second-guess
Where others would have balked.
To stop and think when at the brink
Could cost them victims' lives.
They made a prayer that God would spare
The grieving of their wives. [11]

In 2008, Tom Kenney was a 35-year veteran and Fire Captain on the Providence Fire Department.

Ten Seconds With God
Tom Kenney, 2004

Ten seconds is a very long time
When that's all you have to live
Time enough to make your peace
But not enough to give…

To give your honey one more kiss
To squeeze her oh so tight
To give your kids assurance that
Everything will be all right

From the moment I began this job
I've prepared for this day
So now, as He calls me home
It seems I know the way

Kaboom, kaboom, kaboom, kaboom
Like a freight train bearing down
I instantly knew how this would end
And I felt His peace surround...

Surround my body, and my soul
Surround my brothers in arms
I felt His love, like a giant cloak
Sheltering us from harm

While answering the call that day
I saw the second plane
It glided through the cloudless sky
Then burst into fiery rain

It rained down fire, rained down dust
It rained down bodies, too
It seemed no matter how we tried
There was nothing we could do

We knew that people trapped above
The hole that ripped the tower
Could never escape, with their lives
Without His awesome power

I prayed that day, a silent prayer
As I stepped inside the lobby
I knew that without His help
We'd only recover bodies

We started up the narrow stairs
While others were heading out
As we passed the scared civilians
Some began to shout...

"God bless you, our brave firemen.
You're heroes to us all."

But we were merely doing our jobs
Answering the call

We knew when we began the fight
We all would not survive
But by risking our lives for others
We keep the dream alive...

The dream that good will conquer all
And God will help us through
Reward us with eternal life
As we begin anew

I saw the face of God that day
As He led me to this place
His will, not ours, will be done
Accept this fact with grace

I understood, at once, that day
What we were sent here for
Watch over each other as best we can
For who could ask for more

Ten seconds is a very long time... [12]

3-4-3

Tom Kenney, 2007

It's funny how people remember us
From that fateful day
As the heroes who climbed the towers
Passing workers on the way

They see the footage of us in the lobby
Preparing for the haul
The look on our faces, they say
Surely says it all

"They knew they were going to die",
They tell each other

"You can see it in their eyes as they
Greet a fellow brother"

They fail to realize it's not uncommon
For us to show our fear
But we never allow the fear to stop us
We just keep each other near

We may be proud, we may be brave
But suicidal, we're not
We take many risks to do our jobs
Giving all we've got

They think we know it's a death sentence
As we enter the lobby door
Unaware that not a man here among us
Had not been here before

As we walk through the valley of death again
That old familiar place
We can't accept that we'll leave our souls
And feel death's cold embrace

If we had known we would never come out
We'd have never gone in
Fearing and knowing are two different things
So we hold our doubts within

As we climbed up the stairs floor by floor
Searching zone by zone
It was saving lives that was on our minds
Not giving up our own

The Angel of Death is our frequent companion
A feared and lethal foe
But when he's here for one of our own
How are we to know

We're trained to push things to the limit
On each and every call
We're well aware that lives are on the line
And we may sacrifice all

We live with this throughout our careers
Through every single shift
It hangs in the air like a shroud of fog
Which we can never set adrift

Some think it's merely words when we say
We risk our lives for you
But we take this fact into account
In everything we do

That day in September in 2001
Was no different in our eyes
We could not have known what devastation
Was raining from the skies

We look down from above as our brothers
Desperately search "the pile"
They have no idea that we're finally at rest
They're still in denial

Our bravery that day seemed beyond belief
In the eyes of humanity
But the fact is we've faced our mortality before
Though you may question our sanity

We were merely men doing the job we loved
Down to our last breaths
We remain merely men in the scheme of it all
Even after our deaths. [13]

The Best of What We Can Be

Tom Kenney, 2007

I know that the "343" of the FDNY
Were the best of what we can be
They gave their lives to do their jobs
But we – I mean I – wonder if I could see...

If I could see the honor in running in
As opposed to running away
I can't hold myself to their bravery
If I'm not up to following their way

I think that I've proven over the years
I can do the job when it gets tough
But I wonder if I could do what they did
And I wonder if that's enough

For a man can only speak for himself
Not presume to represent another
But these men paid the ultimate price
Side by side with their brothers

Some of whom lost their lives that day
Had already ended their tour
But they jumped on the rigs nonetheless
As they motored out the door

They knew they were desperately needed
To mount any type of attack
They headed to the biggest job of their lives
Without ever glancing back

Their jobs, you see, were to protect & serve
Whether on duty or not
For firefighters are always at the ready
To give it their best shot

Danger and death are constant companions
Riding along on every call
But I wonder if those firemen were aware
They'd be claimed once and for all

This is the question I must ask myself
Could I have climbed aboard?
Knowing full well the risk I'd be taking
And what I was rushing toward

If the answer is no, I must reassess
The reasons that I'm here

For if I'm not willing to risk my life
I shouldn't don the gear

I believe I'm willing to step up to the plate
And do what needs to be done
Whenever it is I may be called upon
To answer that type of run

I hope and pray it never comes to that
At least not by choice
But we – I mean I – prepare just the same
For the job that silences my voice

I think that might be part of the reason
I write about death so much
Preparing myself for the inevitable end
When it holds me in its clutch

Far too many lives, and deaths, go unnoticed
As if they didn't matter
When St. Peter asks if I was timid or brave
I hope I can answer the latter. [14]

Chapter Nine

Where was God on 9/11/2001?

Every parting is a form of death,
as every reunion is a type of heaven. [1]

Tryon Edwards
American Theologian, 1809-1894
Great Grandson of Johnathan Edwards

When things are well in life, God becomes an afterthought (Luke 17:17 Jesus Christ heals 10 diseased men. Only **one** thanks Him.), but when massive tragedy and death come a-knocking outside our control, God is likely to be put at the forefront of blame.

The America our forefathers originally built on Christ-centered individual soul liberty has been dying a slow death of national suicide spawned by a pop cultural "rock-n-roll rebellion" in the 1950s meant to challenge, then wave bye-bye to society's centerpiece of freedom - Biblical morals – being governed by God's law from within.

The boundary-pushing filth American culture wallows in naturally shoves God further and further out. Amoral "rights" have washed over decades of generational youth with acidic results, until America's Christian nucleus today is on life support, barely visible, as we launch into a new millennium.

We've damned God in our hearts and mocked God with our lives. American youth-now-adults were reared giving Godly mores "the finger" through raunchy music, twisted video games, mindless-twit sitcoms, comedic political correctness, and subtly vicious movie productions villianizing traditionally-honored Christian virtues. They now put God "on trial" whenever national disaster occurs. It exhibits the zenith of American spiritual naiveté.

At the blush of dawn on 9/11/2001, God was ready for a day of national disaster, though He would not stop it. Why? You see, God does not interfere with man's free will - ever. If the world wants to blow itself up, if you want to blow yourself up, God lets us decide our own actions and allows natural law consequences.

God does not impose His will. He reacts. God reacts, when our actions align to *His* Word. His help is ever present, if we but ask.

Many people recorded testimonies of "providential hindrances" which prevented them from being in the World Trade Center on the morning of 9/11/2001, definitely saving their lives. ..God?

Can you recall WTC survivor Lauren Manning's story described earlier in Chapter 3(p.72) In my best "Paul Harvey voice"..*now here's the rest of the story.* Lauren's husband, Greg, planned to attend a breakfast conference at Windows on the World, the restaurant atop the World Trade Center. At the last minute, he changed his mind to help out a friend, who had recent foot surgery, to go vote in that day's primary election. The breakfast conference would seal the fate of all of Greg's associates in attendance.

Lauren and Greg's lives were <u>both</u> saved on 9/11. ..God?

Akin to the struggle of death and life itself, for every story of loss, there are stories of salvation, if your eyes are open to see it.

The author personally spoke with WTC survivor, Manuel Chea, during several phone interviews, and possesses a video copy of Mr. Chea's testimonied account of how God spared his life, as he escaped the North Tower just before it came crashing down. ..God? (Chea's video was shown during a 10th Year Commemoration of 9/11 event hosted by the author and his father on 9/11/2011 at the Lexington Civic Center in North Carolina.)

How could WTC survivor, Mr. Buzzelli, account for being "bounced around on air" like on a roller coaster, as he describes it, "surfing" down 15 stories to safety from the 22nd floor? - as the North Tower came crashing to the ground - which we have all seen on video, and we all know it looks virtually impossible to survive. ..God?

How about WTC survivors Sujo and Mary John? All 110 stories of the South Tower collapsed around Sujo as he was standing near the foot of the building. The debris of the building was falling all around. Sujo and the people around him huddled together at one end of the building. He prayed for protection under the blood of Jesus and asked God to give him strength.

Sujo looked up after the building's collapse (which we have all seen on video) and found himself in three feet of white soot and glass, but no debris fell on him. When he got to his feet, it was eerily silent. Then, he saw dead bodies all around him, but he was still alive, surviving an avalanche of concrete death. ..God?

Mary missed being on time for work because her train arrived at the World Trade Center subway stop late, just five minutes after the first crash. ..God?

Famed evangelist Billy Graham's daughter, Anne Graham Lotz, was interviewed on *CBS*'s *The Early Show* by Jane Clayson who asked (regarding the attacks on 9/11/2001):

Clayson:
*I've heard people say, those who are religious, those who are not, if God is good, **how could God let this happen**? To that, you say?..*

Graham Lotz:
I say God is also angry when he sees something like this. I would say also for several years now Americans in a sense have shaken their fist at God and said, **God, we want you out** *of our schools, our government, our business, we want you out of our marketplace. And* **God, who is a gentleman, has just quietly backed out** *of our national and political life, our public life. Removing his hand of blessing and protection. We need to turn to God first of all and say, God, we're sorry we have treated you this way and we invite you now to come into our national life. We put our trust in you. We have our trust in God on our coins, we need to practice it.* [2]

God was discouraging people from taking the four doomed flights of 9/11/2001. Together they could accommodate more than 1,000 passengers, yet there were approximately only 266 aboard.

God was on those four flights giving terrified passengers the ability to stay calm. Not one of the people who were phoned by a loved one on one of the hijacked planes mentioned passengers being panicked - scared..yes - hysterical..no; nor was there any mindless screaming in the background. And, on one of the flights, God gave utmost strength to passengers who fought back to overcome the hijackers. ..God?

"Someone/something" was busy creating more obstacles than usual to prevent people who worked in the WTC from getting to work on time. When an average work day began, more than 50,000 people worked in the two towers, yet only 18,000 were at their desks on 9/11/2001. On that beautiful morning, scores of unexpected traffic delays, subway delays, and commuter train delays, prevented people from arriving at the WTC on time. A PATH train packed with commuters was stopped at a "malfunctioned" signal just short of the WTC and was able to return to Jersey City.[3] ..God?

"Something" held up the two mighty towers for roughly 90 minutes, until most occupants were able to exit the buildings. The towers fell inward, rather than topple over and outward, which would have killed so many more people. The foundations of six surrounding buildings were demolished, but they held up for hours, until all were completely evacuated. ..God?

People previously trained to deal with disaster crisis and preparedness, such as Mayor Rudy Giuliani, were already in place with skill to act clearly and concisely and save many that were injured, as well as lead into recovery relief. Thousands of others were "called in" to help in any way they were needed, such as 9/11 hero, David Karnes, who felt God's call in Connecticut to assist in recovery efforts, driving furiously to Ground Zero all night long, then locating the final two survivors in the WTC rubble. ..God?

People were brought together across the world in a way that moved thousands to tears and hundreds of thousands to prayer, causing millions to turn to seeking God.

See the heart-warming video from September 11, 2001, when both Republican and Democrat members of the US Congress spontaneously joined together in singing "God Bless America" on the steps of the US Capitol: ..only God could manage that! **www.youtube.com/watch?v=LF_6X2kU8WM**

More documented accounts of people who were, perhaps, providentially hindered from going to the WTC on 9/11/2001: The head of one company survived because he took his son to kindergarten. Another fellow is alive because it was his turn to bring donuts. Another lady was late because her alarm clock didn't go off on time. One was late as a result of being stuck on the NJ Turnpike because of an auto accident. One more survivor missed his bus. One spilled food on her clothes and had to take time to change. One's car wouldn't start. One went back to answer the telephone. One had a child that dawdled and didn't get ready as soon as he should have. One couldn't get a taxi. One man who put on a new pair of shoes that morning, went to work by his usual way but before he got there, he developed a blister on his foot. So he stopped at a drugstore to buy a Band-Aid. That is why he is alive today. ..God?

Monica O'Leary thought her luck had taken a turn for the worse on Monday afternoon when she got laid off from her job. But the fact that she didn't go to work on Tuesday turned out to be nothing short of miraculous for Ms. O'Leary. She had worked as a software saleswoman for eSpeed Inc., a technology company with offices on the 105th floor of the World Trade Center. Ms. O'Leary, 23, is still grappling with memories of her last visit with co-workers on Monday afternoon. *"I worked with a lot of guys, so I kissed them on the cheek and said goodbye,"* she says. *"Little did I know that it was really goodbye."* [4] ..God?

Greer Epstein worked at the Morgan Stanley & Co. offices on the 67th floor of the World Trade Center. He escaped disaster by slipping out of the building for a cigarette just before a 9am staff meeting. ..God?

Bill Trinkle, of Westfield, N.J., had planned to get an early start on his job as sales manager for Trading Technologies Inc., a software corporation with offices on the 86th floor of the World Trade Center's [North] Tower One. But after fussing with his two-year-old daughter and hanging curtains in her bedroom, he missed the train that would have gotten him into the office about a half hour before the attack. Instead, he took a later train elsewhere to visit a client company, where workers hugged him as soon as he walked through the door. [5] ..God?

Joe Andrew, a Washington lawyer and former chairman of a Democratic National Committee, had a ticket for seat 6-C on the ill-fated American Airlines Flight 77 from Dulles International Airport to Los Angeles, but switched to a later flight at the last minute. *"I happen to be a person of faith,"* says Mr. Andrew, *"but even if you aren't, anybody who holds a ticket for a flight that went down ... will become a person of faith."* [6]

On this day, "bad luck" actually turned into "good luck." Nicholas Reihner was upset when he twisted his ankle while hiking during a vacation to Bar Harbor, Maine. But it was the reason he missed his Tuesday morning trip home to Los Angeles from Boston on the American Airlines flight that was hijacked and crashed into the World Trade Center. *"After I sprained my ankle, I was bellyaching to my hiking companion about how life sucks,"* says the 33-year-old legal assistant. *"I feel now that life has never been sweeter. It's great to be alive."* [7] ..God?

A-list actor Mark Wahlberg was born and raised near Boston, Massachusetts. He went on to star in such films as "The Perfect Storm", "Invincible", and "Transformers." On September 11, 2001, he and some friends were scheduled to fly on American Airlines Flight 11, from Boston to Los Angeles. At the last minute they changed their plans and decided to charter a plane to Toronto, Canada, for a film festival. From Toronto, they flew on to Los Angeles. Wahlberg admits his brush with death still haunts his dreams. ..God?

Then there's George Keith, a Pelham, N.Y., investment banker who had a meeting at 9am Tuesday on the 79th floor of the World Trade Center. While he was driving through Central Park the night before, however, the transmission of Mr. Keith's brand-new BMW sport-utility vehicle got stuck in first gear. The breakdown forced him to cancel the morning meeting. But by the time he called the BMW dealer Tuesday, he was anything but furious. *"I told them it was the best transmission problem I'll ever have,"* he said.[8] ..God?

David Gray, a compliance officer for Washington Square Securities, lives in Princeton, N.J., and was due to arrive by commuter train at the World Trade Center for a meeting with one of the firm's brokers just as the first plane hit. But a few days earlier, Mr. Gray, the husband of New York City Ballet principal ballerina Kyra Nichols, broke his foot while jumping rope at home. Mr. Gray said he had been feeling very "sheepish" about the nature of the accident, but now says, *"Thank God I was a lousy jump-roper."* After he broke his foot, he rescheduled the meeting for later in the day so that he could drive into Manhattan instead of taking the commuter train. *"So I was on the New Jersey Turnpike watching the World Trade Center go up in flames, instead of being in it."* [9] ..God?

For Irshad Ahmed and the employees of his Pure Energy Corp., the circumstances were these: A postponed meeting, a delay at a child's school, and a quick stop at the video store. Mr. Ahmed, president of the motor-fuels maker, had been set to attend a 9am meeting in the company's 53rd floor conference room inside [North] Tower One. But the week before, the participants decided to push the meeting back. As a result, none of Pure Energy's nine employees were at work when the planes struck. Some were at a New Jersey lab. Others were out at appointments. Mr. Ahmed's secretary was running late at her child's school. As for Mr. Ahmed, he decided to stop off and return a couple of Blockbuster videos. *"It's one of those little decisions you make that lead up to big events in life,"* he says. [10] ..God?

A chance meeting between actress Gwyneth Paltrow and a total stranger, Lara Lundstrom Clarke, saved Clarke's life. Both had been exercising that morning, Paltrow taking in an early yoga class, Clarke rollerblading along the Hudson.

While Clarke was crossing in the middle of a West Village street in New York, Paltrow was driving in her silver Mercedes SUV. Suddenly, Clarke looked over and realized who was in the SUV. Clarke and Paltrow each stopped and the two of them exchanged greetings. This small delay made Clarke miss her train to the World Trade Center South Tower, where she worked on the 77th floor. At the time Clarke recalled being excited to tell her coworkers who she had just seen. She caught the next train and stepped off the platform just in time to see the first plane fly into Tower One. ..God?

Marianne McInerney, executive director of the National Business Travel Association, would have been on the doomed American Airlines Flight 11 from Dulles to Los Angeles if not for a last-minute flight change. Ms. McInerney, a stickler for not paying more than $1,000 for business flights, had reluctantly booked a ticket on the ill-fated flight. But, she managed to find a less expensive ticket out of Washington's National Airport on a different flight. [11] ..God?

The Duchess of York, Sarah Ferguson, was in New York City on September 11, 2001. She was at the *NBC* studios being interviewed by Matt Lauer when the first plane hit. Ferguson's charity, "Chances for Children," was located on the 101st floor of WTC North Tower 1. She was scheduled to be in the building with the charity but she was running late. Though none of the charity's employees were trapped in the building, nearly 700 employees of Cantor Fitzgerald, the financial firm providing free office space to the duchess' charity, unfortunately perished. ..God?

Marya Gwadz can thank her unborn son for being away from her 16th story office in [South] Tower Two. Ms. Gwadz, 37, a principal investigator for the nonprofit National Development Research Institute, usually gets to work as early as 8:45 each morning. But on Tuesday, being 8½ months pregnant with her first child, she was feeling tired, so she caught a later subway from her Brooklyn apartment, and got out at an early stop. *"It was a beautiful stop and a beautiful day,"* she recalls. Then she saw the flames, and later watched her own building crumble. *"At that point, I grabbed my stomach and started to run,"* she says. [12] ..God?

Steve Scheibner was scheduled to pilot AA Flight 11 on the morning of 9/11/2001. Instead, a pilot with more seniority bumped him out of the pilot rotation, sparing his life. See *In My Seat*: **https://www.youtube.com/watch?v=cLj4akmncsA&feature=youtu.be**

Animator of the TV cartoon hit "Family Guy," Seth McFarlane has made millions of Americans laugh over crass humor. If it had not been for a mix up in his travel itinerary on September 11, 2001, MacFarlane would never have had the chance to create "American Dad!" or "The Cleveland Show."

On September 11, 2001, he was scheduled to return to Los Angeles on American Airlines Flight 11, after delivering a keynote speech at his alma mater, the Rhode Island School of Design, in Rhode Island. Fortunately for MacFarlane, his travel agent told him his flight would leave Logan Airport at 8:15am, when it was actually scheduled to depart at 7:45am.

MacFarlane arrived at Boston Logan Airport a few minutes after boarding was stopped on his AA Flight 11, and he was told he would have to wait for the next flight. An hour later, AA Flight 11 was flown into the North Tower of the World Trade Center, killing everyone on the plane. MacFarlane quickly contacted his parents after the plane hit the WTC to tell them he was not on it and was alive. ..God?

Convicted of a 1986 robbery and killing, Texas inmate Jeffrey Eugene Tucker was scheduled to be executed Tuesday evening, September 11, 2001. Instead, he got a last-minute, 30-day stay from TX Governor Rick Perry because the US Supreme Court was closed, preventing last-minute appeals. Tucker was executed by lethal injection November 14, 2001. In the 30 day reprieve, Tucker refused more appeals for life in prison against the advice of his attorney, was able to set his affairs in order with God, and apologize to the victim's family, stating that he hoped his death would provide some solace to the victim's family.

Many victims who perished in the 9/11 attacks met God for the first time, calling on His name to save them while facing certain death situations. Romans 10:13 says, *For whosoever shall call upon the name of the Lord, **shall be saved**.* And for those who did ask God to save them, their souls took flight to the heavens, forever resting in perfection with a mighty Savior, Jesus Christ.

Though there is no magic wand, nor secret pill, to erase the memory or pain caused by the 9/11 attacks, there is divine power available to make something positive out of it. Amazing salvation rests in divine "2nd chance" love. Real grace in the outstretched hand of God the Son, your Creator, Jesus Christ, caresses each infant in Heaven lost at 9/11. Would you like to meet the victims of 9/11 again? You may. Jesus Christ delivers this hope.

Would you like to accept your Father's free gift of salvation to go to Heaven? Just like many victims and survivors did on 9/11/2001, wholly present yourself to Jesus Christ just as you are right now. He awaits your prayer. Jesus instantly saves a soul. Understand God's simple Plan of Salvation:

1. **Understand the Sinner.**
   We were all born with a sin nature..
   Psalm 51:10 *Behold, I was shapen in iniquity; and in sin did my mother conceive me.*
   Romans 3:23 *For all have **sinned** and come short of the glory of God.*
   Romans 5:12 *Wherefore as by one man, **sin** entered into the world, and death by **sin**, so death passed upon all men, for that **all have sinned**.*
   No one is perfect. Sin separates us from God in this life; also in the eternal life to come. There are only 2 places where people go after death: Heaven, hell. You can choose to pay for your own sins in a real lake of fire and eternal damnation. Or, choose the previous payment of your sins by taking Jesus Christ.

2. **Understand the Sacrifice.**
   Romans 5:8 *But God commendeth his love toward us, in that, while we were yet sinners, **Christ died for us**.*
   "God in skin", Jesus Christ, left Heaven 2,000 yrs ago to live a perfect life on Earth. This world crucified him in a torturous, court-ordered Roman death on a cross. It was His plan to shed sinless blood for payment of **your** sins, so you would not have to pay. You were loved this much before you were even born. Jesus Christ is the only God-man in the history of planet Earth who ever lived, died, was buried in a grave, and rose from the dead. He ascended back up to Heaven 150 days later to complete humanity's salvation plan.

3. **Understand the Saviour.**
   Romans 10:9 *That if thou shalt confess with thy mouth the **Lord Jesus**, and believe in thine heart that God hath raised him from the dead, thou shalt be saved.*

Does it say to confess that you are a good person? No. Does it say confess that you go to church? No. Religious? No. Donate to charity? Live a good life? No. No. God's Word simply states to confess *the Lord Jesus.* It means to vocalize your need for Christ: *"Jesus, you are my need. I want you to be my Saviour."* That's it. No more; no less. Christ Jesus is willing to save any soul from hell for Heaven who simply believes on Him as a personal Saviour.

4. Understand His Salvation.
Romans 10:13 *For whosoever shall call upon the name of the Lord shall be saved.* Who is "whosoever?" You. Me. The very moment you ask Jesus Christ to be *your* Saviour, Heaven becomes your home. Your sins are forgiven. Your soul is secure. Your standing is right with God. Welcome to a new and personal relationship with your Creator! Whosoever means YOU.

John 3:16 – The Breadth, Length, Depth, Height of God's love:
For God so loved the world.. = **Breadth** of God's love.
..that he gave his only begotten son = **Length** of God's love.
..that whosoever believeth in him should not perish = **Depth**
..but have everlasting life. = **Height** of God's love.

Prayer of Salvation:
Dear Father, I understand that I am a sinner. I understand that Jesus died on the cross to pay for my sins, so that I would not have to pay for my own sins in hell. I understand Jesus is the only way to Heaven, according to your Holy Word. Dear Jesus, please forgive my sins. Please, come into my heart and save my soul. I am trusting in you. Thank you for your forgiveness and love for me. Thank you for my eternal home in Heaven. Amen.

To further understand how to go to Heaven, you may watch a brief video presentation at **troyclark.net**, or download my FREE eBook: *Email From God,* at **smashwords.com**; or watch my YouTube video: "God's Salvation Plan", **youtube.com/watch?v=kPHiKrm9faw**.

The fact that an estimated 50,000 people on average worked at the World Trade Center towers, and altogether 140,000 visited the complex daily, is rarely compared to the 18,000 workers in the WTC towers when terrorist-controlled airliners struck the buildings on 9/11/2001. Roughly 15,000 made it out alive after the planes hit, while roughly 3,000 souls perished.[13] Four times as many survived the attacks than died.

Reality begs us to notice the sheer number of fatalities **could** easily have been much, much higher were it not for an "unseen hand" of divine Providence directing WTC workers *away* from the Twin Towers circumstantially in literally tens of thousands of individual lives that were spared.

Islamic terrorists managed to find a weakness in our nation. They also exposed our strength. They shocked our way of life, but also awakened our resolve to become better. They killed our citizens, but not our spirit. While targeting our tallest extremities, they missed our nation's soul.

Islamic terrorists sought to bring America to its knees. That they did successfully, not in submissive defeat, but to seek the Almighty more in prayer - - the heart of America's power.

When the world asks, *"Where was God on 9/11?"* look to an American flag draped over a building railing, while people gather together with bowed heads. Look to videos of people flooding churches months after the crisis. Look to memorial vigils with people holding candles in contemplation of victims given over to the afterlife. Look to songs, poems, monuments, books, works of art, films, and creative expressions of God's strength, mercy, and grace in America.

Yes, God **was** there, listening, taking action, keeping His promise to never leave us, nor forsake us (Hebrews 13:5). This is the whole 9/11 story, its untold truth, no one can blow apart.

Israeli 9/11 Memorial

It is called the **9/11 Living Memorial Plaza**. Completed in 2009 for $2 million, it sits on 5 acres of hillside, 20 miles from the center of Jerusalem. The site solemnly overlooks Jerusalem's largest cemetery, Har HaMenuchot. The memorial is a 30-foot, bronze American flag that forms the shape of a flame to commemorate over 3,000 lives lost in the flames of all 9/11 attacks. The base of the monument is made of melted steel from the wreckage of the World Trade Center. Surrounding the monument are plaques with names of 9/11 victims. It is the only memorial outside the US that includes the names of all victims who perished in the terrorist attacks, including 5 Israeli citizens.

Endnotes

Chapter One:
1. Michelle Malkin, "All the wrong 9/11 lessons", *michellemalkin.com,* 9/9/2011, p.1.
2. Ergun Caner, *Unveiling Islam,* 2001, p.183.
3. Dan Collins, "99 report warned of suicide hijacking", *cbsnews.com,* 5/17/2002, p.1.
4. "Al-Shifa Pharmaceutical factory", *Wikipedia.com,* 10/2/2015, p.1.
5. Dan Good, "Bill Clinton, Hours before 9/11 attack: 'I could have killed' Osama bin Laden", *abcnews.go.com,* 8/1/2014, p.1.

Chapter Two:
1. Michael Walters, "A day we will never forget", *9/11 Memorial Website,* 10/5/2015, p.1.
2. Tim Thornsberg, "Many eyewitnesses saw Flight 93", 911research.wtc7.net, 9/9/2015, p.1.
3. Mark Elsis, "The most comprehensive minute by minute timeline on 9/11", *http://911timeline.net/,* 9/9/2002, p. 5-32.
    Paul Thompson, "Flight 93 Timeline", *fromthewilderness.com,* 10/6/2015, p.2-13.
4. Emily Ngo, "9/11 memorial honors unborn babies", *newsday.com,* 9/1/2011, p.4.
5. Washingtons blog, "9/11: The mystery collapse of WTC building 7 was not an inside job", *washingtonsblog.com,* 9/15/2012, p.8.
6. Ibid, p.7
7. The Survivor's Circle, "Eight who were there meet and compare lives", New York News and Politics, *mymag.com,* p.1.

Chapter Three:
1. Danny Cox, "Remembering 9/11: Quotes that will help everyone never forget," *examiner.com,* 9/10/2013, p.1.
2. "Dave Karnes", *Wikipedia.com,* 9/13/2015, p.2.
3. Rebecca Liss, "An unlikely hero", *slate.com,* 9/11/2015, p.2.
4. Ibid, p.2.
5. Ibid, p.2.
6. Alison Matas, "9/11 rescuer recounts path from Connecticut to World Trade Center," *cantonrep.com,* 9/11/2014, p.2.
7. "Dave Karnes", *Wikipedia.com,* 9/13/2015, p.3.
8. Manuel Chea, "9/11video testimony of Manuel Chea", Lexington Civic Center 9/11 event, 9/11/2011.
9. Robert Tomsho, Barbara Carton, "Lucky among the ruins", *swapmeetdave.com & The Wall Street Journal,* Sept.2001, p.2.
10. Laura Donnelly, "9/11 survivor tells how he 'surfed' 15 floors down the collapsing tower", *telegraph.co.uk,* 9/8/2012, p.1.
11. Ibid, p.1.

12. Bob Minzesheimer, "Survivor Lauren Manning finds new normal after 9/11", *usatoday30.usatoday.com,* 8/29/2011, p.2.
13. Ibid, p.3.
14. David W. Dunlap, Nate Schweber, "In a 9/11 survival tale, the pieces just don't fit", *wtcdemolition.com,* 9/27/2007, p.2.

Chapter Four:
1. Bill Federer, "The long history of September 11 Muslim atrocities", *wnd.com,* 9/10/2015, p.2.
2. Ibid, p.2.
3. Pastor David L. Brown, Ph.D, "The Aitken Bible", *logosresourcepages.org,* 2012, p.1.
4. Michael D. Shear, "Benghazi panels engages Clinton in tense session", *nytimes.com,* 10/22/2015, p.5.
5. "Emails reportedly show confidant told Clinton Benghazi attack planned by fighters tied to al Qaeda", *foxnews.com,* p.2.
6. Ibid, p.2.
7. Bill Gertz, "US seeking al Qaeda terrorist linked to Benghazi attack", *freebeacon.com,* 1/3/2014, p.3,4.

Chapter Five:
1. Anthony Saltalamacchia, "9/11 survivors and family members question the 9/11 Commission Report", *patriotquestions911.com,* 10/2/2015, Arthur DelBianco, p.9.
2. Louie Cacchioli, "A personal history", *louiecacchioli.com/about.html,* 10/6/2015, p.2.
3. Washingtons blog, "9/11: The mysterious collapse of WTC Building 7 was not an inside job", *washingtonsblog.com,* 9/15/2012, p.3.
4. Ibid, p.2.
5. Ibid, p.3
6. Graham John Inman, "WTC 7 Gallery of evidence", *ae911truthorg,* 10/2/2015, p.2.
7. Washingtonsblog, "9/11: The mysterious collapse of WTC Building 7 was not an inside job", *washingtonsblog.com,* 9/15/2012, p.4.
8. Ibid, p.5.
9. Ibid, p.5.
10. Kamal S, Obeid, "WTC 7 Gallery of evidence", *ae911truthorg,* 10/2/2015, p.1.
11. Ibid, p.1.
12. Anthony Saltalamacchia, "9/11 survivors and family members question the 9/11 Commission Report", *patriotquestions911.com,* 10/2/2015, p.4.
13. Ibid, Philip Morelli, p.4.
14. Ibid, Marlene Cruz, p.6.
15. Ibid, Mike Pecoraro, p.7.
16. William Rodriguez, "9/11 survivors and family members question the 9/11 Commission Report", *patriotquestions911.com,* 10/2/2015, p.1.

17. Ibid, Felipe David, p.10.
18. Ibid, Hursley Lever, p.11.
19. Bill Grady, *How Satan Turned America Against God,* 2005, p.705.
20. Ibid, p.705
21. Ibid, p.706.
22. Ibid, p.708.
23. Ibid, p.708
24. Ibid, p.708.
25. Ibid, p.708.
26. Ibid, p.711.
27. Ed Vulliamy, "Let's Roll", *the guardian.com,* 12/1/2001, p.1.
28. Ibid, p.1.
29. Ibid, p.2.
30. Ibid, p.2.
31. Paul Wolfowitz, "Interview transcript with Margaret Warner", *pbs.org,* 9/14/2001, p.2.
32. "Rumsfeld says 9-11 plane 'shot down' in Pennsylvania", *wnd.com,* 12/27/2004, p.1.
33. William Bunch, "Flight 93: We know it crashed, but not why", *whatreallyhappened.com,* 11/15/2001, p.1.
34. Ibid, p.3.
   "Many eyewitnesses saw Flight 93", 911research.wtc7.net, 9/9/2015, p.1.
35. Ibid, p.2.
36. Ibid, p.2.
37. "Rumsfeld says 9-11 plane 'shot down' in Pennsylvania", *wnd.com,* 12/27/2004, p.1.
38. Paul Thompson, "Flight 93 Timeline", *fromthewilderness.com,* 10/6/2015, p.13.
39. Ibid, p.2-13.
40. Ibid, p.2-13
41. Ibid, p.4.
42. Ibid. p.10.
43. Ibid, p.11.
44. Ibid, p.14.
45. William Bunch, "Flight 93: We know it crashed, but not why", *whatreallyhappened.com,* 11/15/2001, p.5-6.
46. Ibid, p.2.
47. Ibid, p.6.
48. Ray Sanchez, "Plans for mosque near Ground Zero draw outrage in New York", *abcnews.go.com,* 5/18/2010, p.1.
49. Verena Dobnik, "Ground Zero mosque developer regrets not involving 9/11 families", *huffingtonpost.com,* 9/21/2011, p.1.

50. AP New York, "Possible human remains from 9/11 found in new World Trade Center debris, *cbsnews.com*, 4/3/2013, p.2.

51. Dave Lindorff, "Did the Bush administration lie to Congress and the 9/11 Commission?", *911truth.org*, 12/20/2005, p.4.

Chapter Six:

1. Danny Cox, "Remembering 9/11: Quotes that will help everyone never forget," *examiner.com*, 9/10/2013, p.1.

2. John Solomon, "Bill Clinton White House suppressed evidence of Iran's terrorism", *washingtontimes.com*, 10/5/2015, p.1.

3. Gary Satanovsky, "President Bush announces war on terror", *famousdaily.com*, 9/20/2001, p.1.

4. "Words of Mass Destruction", *snopes.com*, 2003, p.2-14.

5. Ibid.

6. Ibid.

7. "Kerry Quotes", *davidstuff.com*, 10/7/2015, p.1.

8. "Words of Mass Destruction", *snopes.com*, 2003, p.2-14.

9. Ibid.

10. Ibid.

11. Ibid.

12. Ibid.

13. Larry Elder, "The WikiLeaks vindication of George W. Bush", *townhall.com*, 12/9/2010, p.1.

14. Ibid, p.2.

15. Ibid, p.2.

16. Joel Roberts, "CBS Poll: Vets favor Bush", *cbsnews.com*, 6/4/2004, p.2-5.

17. "Military causalities during the Bill Clinton administration", *americaswatchtower.com*, 2/20/2007, p.1.

18. Joe Miller, "Military death under Clinton and Bush", *factcheck.org*, 1/29/2008, p.1-2.

19. Allen West, "US Military death in Afghanistan skyrocket under Obama", *allenbwest.com*, 2/13/2004, p.1.

20. Ibid, p.2.

21. Tony Lee, "Media ignores increased deaths, casualties in Afghanistan under Obama", *Breitbart.com*, 9/11/2012, p.2.

22. Edwin Mora, "1,188 US military deaths in Afghan War since Obama became President", *cnsnews.com*, 1/3/2012, p.1.

23. "Khalid Sheikh Mohammed", *en.wikipedia.org/wiki/Khalid_Sheikh_Mohammed*, 10/7/2015, p.1-2.
   Philip Zelikow, "The 9/11 Plot" transcript, *webcitation.org*, 6/16/2004, p.1.

24. "Khalid Sheikh Mohammed", *en.wikipedia.org/wiki/Khalid_Sheikh_Mohammed*, 10/7/2015, p.1-2.

25. Ibid, p.1.

26. Wikiquote, "John Ashcroft", Cal Thomas interview Nov. 2001, en.wikiquote.org, 2/16/2015, p.1.

27. Eleanor Clift, "The Missing Pages of the 9/11 Report", thedailybeast.com, 1/12/2015, p.1.

28. Ira Stoll, "Iraq's WMD secreted in Syria, Sada says", nysun.com, 1/26/2006, p.1.

Chapter Seven:

1. Transcript, "President Bush on 3 month anniversary of the terrorist attacks on the World Trade Center and the Pentagon", *washingtonpost.com*, 12/11/2001, p.1.

2. Ed Vulliamy, "Let's Roll", *theguardian.com*, 12/1/2001, p.1.

3. "Death of Osama bin Laden", *Wikipedia.com*, 10/7/2015, p.12.

4. Ibid, p.13.

5. Frank Newport, Gallup Poll: "Americans back bin Laden mission, CIA most", *gallup.com*, 5/3/2011, p.1.

6. Elizabeth Flock, "Osama bin Laden tells his children not fight jihad in his will", *washingtonpost.com*, 5/4/2011, p.1.

7. Alexander Mullany and Syeda Amna Hassan, "He led the CIA to bin Laden – and unwittingly fueled a vaccine backlash", *nationalgeoegraphic.com*, 2/27/2015, p.14.

8. Frank Newport, "Americans back bin Laden mission; Credit military, CIA most", *gallup.com*, 5/3/2011, p.1.

9. "Zero Dark Thirty", *Wkipedia.com*, 10/15/2015, p.1,11.

10. Jim Hoft, "Judge who sentenced Sadam Hussein to death – captured & executed by ISIS", *thegatewaypundit.com*, 6/22/2014, p.1.

Chapter Eight:

1. Kevin Mills, Sept. 11 Memorial Service, Welcome and Invocation, Heroes Garden, 9/9/2005, p.2.

2. "9/11 Poems", *celebrate-american-holidays.com*, 2002, p.1.

3. Ibid, p.2.

4. Ibid, p.6.

5. Ibid, p.7.

6. Ibid, p.8.

7. Cristin O'Keefe Aptowicz, "WTC 9/11", *allyourprettywords.tumblr.com*, 2013, p.1-2.

8. Ibid, "Silence (over Manhattan)", 2013, p.1.

9. Michael Brett, "9/11 poem from London", *whyareweiniraq.com*, 12/31/2009, p.1.

10. David McLansky, "9/11 Poem", *poemhunter.com*, 10/7/2015, p.1-2.

11. Author Unknown, "Bravery of the Firefighters, *september11thpoem.wordpress.com*, June 2008, p.1.

12. Tom Kenney, "Ten seconds with God", *my.firefighternation.com*, 7/28/2007, p.1.

13. Ibid, p.1-2.

14. Tom Kenney, "The best of what we can be", *theprovidencefireman.blogspot.com,* 2007, p. 6-8.

Chapter Nine:

1. Tryon Edwards, "Heaven Quotes", *brainyquote.com,* 10/7/2015, p.1.

2. The Early Report CBS News, "Where is God?", *web.archive.org,* 9/13/2001, p.1-3.

3. Tess Haranda, "Where was God on 9/11?", *swapmeetdave.com,* 2006, p.1-2.

4. Robert Tomsho, Barbara Carton, Jerry Guidera, "Where was God on 9/11", *swapmeetdave.com,* Sept.2001, p.1-2.

5. Ibid.

6. Ibid.

7. Ibid.

8. Ibid.

9. Ibid.

10. Ibid.

11. Ibid.

12. Ibid.

13. In-depth Special, "War Against Terror", CNN News, cnn.com/specials, 5/10/2016, p.1.

Bibliography

Anschutz, Ann, Anschutz Entertainment Group, examiner.com, Denver, CO, 1994.

Annenberg, Walter and Leonore, Annenberg Public Policy Center, factcheck.org, University of Pennsylvania, Washington, D.C., 2003.

Baker, Gerard, Wall Street Journal, wsj.com, New York, NY, 1889.

Barclay, David and Fredrick, Telegraph Media Group, my.telegraph.co.uk, London, England, 2004.

Barnum, Dan, Architects and Engineers for 9/11 Truth, ae911truth.org, Berkeley, CA, 3/29/2016.

Beasley, Larry, The Washington Times, washingtontimes.com, Washington, D.C., 1982.

Bozell III, Brent, Cybercast News Service, cnsnews.com, Reston, VA, 1998.

Breitbart, Andrew, Breitbart.com, Los Angeles, CA, 2007.

Brown, Dr. David, Logos Communication Consortium, Inc., Oak Creek, WI, 2012.

Brown, Tina, The Daily Beast, IAC, thedailybeast.com, New York, NY, 2008.

Cacchioli, Louie, louiecacchioli.com, Queens, NY, 2016.

Caner, Ergun, Unveiling Islam, Grand Rapids, MI, Kregel Publications, 3/1/2002, 2009.

Cooper, Charles S, Why Are We in Iraq?, whyareweiniraq.com, 2006.

Dennis, Steve, America's Watchtower, americaswatchtower.com, NH, 2013.

Elsis, Mark, 911 Timeline, 911timeline.net, 2002.

Eysenbach, Gunter, Webcite, webcitation.org, Toronto, Canada, 1997.

Farah, Joseph, World Net Daily, wnd.com, Washington, D.C., 1997.

Gallup, George, Gallup Inc, gallup.com, Washington, D.C., 1935.

Garthwaite, Johnathan, Townhall.com, Salem Media Group, Camarillo, CA, 1995.

Goldfarb, Michael, The Washington Free Beacon, freebeacon.com, Washington DC, 2012.

Grady, William P, *How Satan Turned America Against God*, Grady Publications, Knoxville, TN, 2005.

Kerger, Paula, PBS, pbs.org, Arlington County, VA, 1970.

Knell, Gary, national geographic Society, nationalgeographic.com, Washington DC, 1888.

Hoffman, Jim, 9/11 Research, 911research.wtc7.net/about/index.html, Oakland, CA, 2003.

Hoft, Jim, The Gateway Pundit, thegatewaypundit.com, 2004.

Huffington, Arianna, The Huffington Post Media Group, huffingtonpost.com, New York, NY, 2005.

Kinsley, Michael, Slate Magazine, slate.com, New York, NY, 1996.

Lipsky, Seth, New York Sun, nysun.com, New York, NY, 2002.

Malkin, Michelle, Fox News contributor, michellemalkin.com, Dallas, Texas, 3/29/2016.

Matthews, Janice, 911truth.org, Kansas City, KS, 2002.

McLeod, Gordon, Newsday, newsday.com, Melville, NY, 1940.

Mikkelson, Barbara & David P, Urban Legends Reference Pages, Snopes.com, San Fernando Valley, CA, 1995.

Miller, Alan, patriotquestions911.com, 2006.

Moonves, Lee, CBS News Broadcasting, cbsnews.com, New York, NY, 1927.

Moss, Adam, New York Magazine, nymag.com, New York, New York, 1968.

Murdoch, Rupert, Fox News Channel, New York, NY, 1996.

National 9/11 Memorial and Museum, 911memorial.org, New York, NY, 2002.

Neuharth, Al, USA Today, usatoday.com, Tysons Corner, VA, 1982.

Raymond, Henry Jarvis, New York Times, nytimes.com, New York, NY, 1851.

Rivero, Michael, What Really Happened, whatreallyhappened.com, Aiea, HI, 2000.

Ruppert, Michael, From The Wilderness Publications, fromthewilderness.com, Asland, OR, 2005.

Ryan, Fred, The Washington Post, washingtonpost.com, Nash Holdings LLC, Washington, D.C., 1877.

Sherwood, Ben, *ABC News,* Disney Media Networks, New York, NY, 1945.

Turner Broadcasting System, CNN, cnn.com, Atlanta, GA, 1980.

Viner, Katharine, The Guardian, theguardian.com, London, England, 1821.

Wales, Jimmy, Wikisource.org / Wikipedia.org / Project Sourceberg / Wikimedia Foundation, San Francisco, CA, 11/23/2003.

West Allen, allenbwest.com, Washington, D.C., 3/29/2016.

White, Chris, The Repository, cantonrep.com, Canton, OH, 1815.

Xplore Inc, brainyquote.com, McKinney, TX, 2001.

Zuesse, Eric, Washington's Blog, Washington'sblog.com, Washington, D.C., 2007.

Contact, More Publications

View All Publications by Dr. Troy Clark:

amazon.com/author/troyclark

troyclark.net

YouTube Video Channel:
youtube.com/user/DrTroyClark

Post a positive review online:
amazon.com/author/troyclark
(click on book title)

Paperback, eBook, Audiobook:

Amazon.com, Kindle, Smashwords, Barnes-n-Nobles Nook,
Apple iBookstore, Sony Reader, Kobo, Palm Doc, Diesel,
Odilo, Tolino, Yuzu, Oyster, Scribd, OverDrive, Flipkart,
Bookworld, Indigo, Buy.com
Aldiko & Stanza (mobile apps),
Audible.com, Apple iTunes,

Made in the USA
Las Vegas, NV
14 April 2021